Knowing God
to Make Him Known

Knowing God
to Make Him Known

Living Out the Attributes of God Cross-Culturally

ED SCHEUERMAN

Foreword by Sherwood G. Lingenfelter

WIPF & STOCK · Eugene, Oregon

KNOWING GOD TO MAKE HIM KNOWN
Living Out the Attributes of God Cross-Culturally

Wipf & Stock
An Imprint of Wipf and Stock Publishers
199 W. 8th Ave., Suite 3
Eugene, OR 97401

www.wipfandstock.com

PAPERBACK ISBN: 978-1-6667-0021-3
HARDCOVER ISBN: 978-1-6667-0022-0
EBOOK ISBN: 978-1-6667-0023-7

04/16/21

Contents

PART 4: RETURN

Foreword

Now Moses . . . led the flock to the far side of the wilderness and came to Horeb, the mountain of God. There the angel of the LORD appeared to him in flames of fire from within a bush. . . . So Moses thought, "I will go over and see this strange sight—why the bush does not burn up." When the LORD saw that he had gone over to look, God called to him from within the bush, "Moses! Moses!" And Moses said, "Here I am." "Do not come any closer," God said. "Take off your sandals, for the place where you are standing is holy ground."

EXOD 3:1–5

ALMOST EVERY YEAR SINCE 2012, Dr. Ed Scheuerman has invited Judith and me to give a lecture for one session of his cultural anthropology classes at Lancaster Bible College. Having both retired from Biola University and Fuller Theological Seminary, we delighted in this opportunity to meet with and to engage young men and women about the joys and challenges of ministering cross-culturally. Sharing with us his syllabus and some of his Powerpoint lecture slides, he invited us to contribute in a specific way to a topic he found essential for young people considering God's mission.

Dr. Ed, as he is known by students, is a joyful person, and his lecture slides were full of fun pictures, illustrations, diagrams, and illustrations that drew attention to specific points he wished to make in each class session. He also always dressed casually, greeting everyone by name, thus making the classroom experience very personal and relational. And he always took off his shoes when he entered the room, so that all of his activity, teaching, and mentoring were done with bare feet.

When Judith and I first experienced this, we concluded that bare feet was cultural baggage that he brought back from years in Thailand as a missionary with Pioneers. We first met him when he enrolled as a graduate student at Biola University's extension in Chiang Mai. We don't remember if he came to Judith's classes with bare feet, but this practice was very common in Thai culture.

However, as I read this book manuscript, I discovered Dr. Ed's deep passion to know God and to live his relationships with others in the presence of the omniscient and omnipresent Creator of the universe, so that he may "make Him known" to his students and to anyone he encounters. It was from this understanding that the mystery of bare feet was resolved. For Dr. Ed, the classroom where he stands is holy ground; he understands that every time he enters that place to engage God's people, the God he knows and worships is there. He is accountable to his God for how he greets and engages students, for what and how he teaches, for openness to the work of the Spirit among students, and to make God known to them in such a way that they will feel God's passion for a lost world, and respond to God's call to participate in God's mission.

This book is also holy ground for Dr. Ed. Each chapter provides an overview of his understanding of what it means to know God and how that knowledge shapes who we are and transforms how we live and serve. In chapter 2, he shares how we are set apart by God for his purpose and that "the first call of the believer is a call to holiness and obedience." He argues that our priority in preparation must be knowing God and experiencing his holiness. Only when we experience God's holiness is it possible for us to grasp fully the meaning of God's grace and mercy and the joy of giving our lives as living sacrifices in his service. Dr. Ed models that holiness and obedience in his classroom, in his family, in his church, and in this book.

The book is a masterful blend of theology about God, the practical relevance of knowing God in one's journey of preparation for cross-cultural ministry, and obedience in following God in the practice of ministry. He begins by showing how God's sovereignty, holiness, and omnipresence lead the seeker through one's call and preparation for ministry. Each chapter takes us readers deeper in our understanding of God and then leads us to understand God's guidance in our missionary journeys. We discover how God's presence and character provide everything needed for a life of ministry and for its conclusion.

Dr. Ed and his beloved Carol have walked this journey with God together, serving as a family in Thailand and as a care team for Pioneers missionaries working there. Years ago, when God called them, Ed and Carol said "Here we are," and God told them to take off their shoes, they were on holy ground. This book is rich with insights from that life experience of walking on holy ground in God's mission, with authentic humility about the joy and sorrows of loving God and loving broken people in a multi-cultural world. The core truth of this volume is that a calling to ministry is wholly about a deeper relationship with God. It is not about what we, God's servants, accomplish, but rather what God accomplishes when we, God's servants, take off our shoes, and, by God's grace, become holy vessels through which God's spirit does God's work.

SHERWOOD G. LINGENFELTER, PhD
Senior Professor of Anthropology
Fuller Theological Seminary, Pasadena, CA

Acknowledgments

WHILE THIS BOOK WAS written during my sabbatical, it has been God's work in my life for the past fifteen years. But I could make the case that this is the result of nearly forty years of ministry.

Throughout all these years, my wife, Carol, has been the one whom God has used to anchor me. My best friend, my teammate, and disc golf partner. Thanks for modeling many of God's attributes to me.

Our daughters—Kara, Rebekah, Grace, and Faith—have seen the good, the bad, and the ugly in my life. And their husbands have joined our journey with enthusiasm and helped to bring us grandchildren! You all have helped me to grow in understanding how God has created me and how I need to continue to grow into the image of Christ.

For more than thirty years, Carol and I have been part of a movement of God—Pioneers, International. This has been made possible, in large measure, through the faithful praying and giving of many. To all of you, thank you for modeling God's faithfulness in providing for his work to be done in and through our lives.

As the African proverb says, "If you want to go fast, go alone. If you want to go far, go with others." We could not have done what we did on the field without the support of our teammates. Our years in southeast Asia were made all the richer by your impact on our lives.

A special word of appreciation to Drs. Sherwood and Judy Lingenfelter, along with Dr. Tom Steffen, for their support of me through my doctoral studies at Biola University. Sherwood, thank you for your patient mentoring of me through the writing of this book.

And, finally, a word of appreciation to my students here at Lancaster Bible College. You have graciously listened to these stories many times. May God bless you as he leads you in his world with his heart for the lost.

Introduction

For nearly thirty years, our family has been involved in cross-cultural ministry. Twenty-three of those years were spent in Southeast Asia with Pioneers,
International. We have served in isolated (from other cross-cultural work-
ers/missionaries) places, and we have served in a community where "you
couldn't swing a dead cat without hitting a missionary." We have seen lives
transformed by Christ, and we have seen relationships shattered by those
who claim to know Christ. We have seen Christians thrive cross-culturally,
and we have seen others who have seemingly lost their faith.

Christians are all too familiar with the dichotomy between "being a
Mary" (sitting at Jesus' feet) and "being a Martha" (being active in ministry).
We have been told that, before we can DO, we first need to BE. And this
is well and good. But it is insufficient. Before we can BE, we first need to
KNOW. We need to KNOW who God is (God's attributes) so that we can
then BE who we are intended to be in Christ. Only then should we seek to
DO what he has called and equipped us to do for his glory.

> Likewise, in order to believe in God—to trust in God—one
> must believe that God exists; but this isn't enough. One also
> needs to know God, to know that God is good, powerful, and
> loving. Only when one knows this will one's trust in God lead
> to doing the will of God . . . . The more we understand God, the
> better we will be able to trust and rest in God. And the more we
> trust God, the better we will understand God.[1]

Psalm 46:10 has become somewhat of a poster-child verse for those
who want to emphasize the being aspect of our spiritual lives. "He says, 'Be

---

1. González, *Knowing Our Faith*, 10.

1

still and know that I am God; I will be exalted among the nations, I will be exalted in the earth.'" The focus is typically on the need to BE. But that misses the main point of this verse. God's will is that he be exalted among all the peoples of the earth, that all would know him. To that end, he calls us to be still so that we can know him. The reason for being still is to focus on who God IS—that is, knowing God in all his glorious attributes. Being still is the means to knowing God. Knowing God, in turn, leads to making him known.

The unique challenge of doing this cross-culturally is the emphasis of this book—being still, knowing God, and making him known. Jesus modeled this ministry in his coming to the world to love the world. My desire is to draw you to an awareness of the need to know God in all of his glorious facets (attributes) so that you can reflect God to the world. The book is ordered chronologically according to the different phases of cross-cultural ministry (preparation, departure, ministry, return), connecting one or more attributes along each step of the journey. As you truly know God, you will— by his grace—live out your knowledge of him, both locally and globally.

WHY DO WE NEED TO KNOW WHAT GOD IS LIKE?

A proper understanding of God is foundational to living a life that attempts to glorify him. According to the Westminster Catechism, the response to the first question (What is the chief end of man?) is "Man's chief end is to glorify God and to enjoy him forever."[2] A study of the attributes of God will help us to enjoy and glorify God.

Many have attempted to list, categorize, and detail the attributes of God. There are many wonderful writings, some of which are used in this book. I have decided to utilize A. W. Tozer's list in *The Attributes of God*, as it is both simple and helpful. The list includes the following attributes, given in order of use in this book:

- Self-existence
- Sovereignty
- Holiness
- Omnipresence
- Faithfulness
- Immutability

2. "Westminster Shorter Catechism."

- Grace
- Mercy
- Wisdom
- Love
- Justice
- Transcendence
- Omnipotence
- Immensity
- Infinitude
- Goodness
- Immanence
- Eternalness
- Omniscience
- Knowable

As each is used, I will discuss the cross-cultural context for utilizing the attribute, its meaning, its scriptural basis for discussion, and how to see it lived out in cross-cultural ministry.

Some have argued that focusing on God's attributes is detrimental to our view of God. "If we distinguish them, it is because of the limitations of our mind."[3] Likewise, others struggle with attempts to categorize the attributes. Snider writes, "I have come to the conclusion that categorizing the attributes of God tends to have subtle effects on the conclusions we draw regarding them, and on the way in which they shape our theologies and lives."[4] We need to be reminded that no one attribute of God stands alone. They work in concert with one another. God is not a combination of attributes. His attributes are ways to understand his nature and how he interacts with us.

Categorizing God's Attributes

This book is not a theological debate about various lists and categories of God's attributes. There are many brilliant writings available for those who would like to pursue those discussions. Because the focus of this book is the living out of God's attributes, I have landed on one of the more common

3. de Poissy, "Chapter II," para. 3.
4. Snider, "Story and System," 1.

categorizations of God's attributes—the two categories of noncommunicable and communicable attributes of God. Noncommunicable means that only God can possess these attributes. For example, only God can be omnipresent. Communicable attributes, like love, are those that can be lived out by us as well, even if not as perfectly as in God. These attributes are sometimes also categorized as his nonmoral and moral attributes, but the former distinction is helpful in that it helps the Christian cross-cultural worker to view each attribute as one in which he either seeks simply to respond to the knowledge of a particular truth (noncommunicable attribute) of God, or to view it as one to additionally seek to emulate (communicable attribute).

Noncommunicable attributes impact the way we see God and the world. Consequently, our actions reveal our understanding of who God is—"The characteristics that God does not share with finite humanity but reserves for Himself alone."[5] Knowing that God is a certain way should inform how we respond to a particular circumstance.

Communicable attributes likewise impact the way we see God and the world. However, with these, we attempt to imitate God. These are attributes that we can more easily understand and live out before others.

> None of these [classifications] has much to commend it and certainly none is to be regarded as authoritative. Scripture nowhere attempts a classification. . . . However, Louis Berkhof justified his use of these categories, saying that, 'if we remember that none of the attributes of God are incommunicable in the sense that there is no trace of them in man, and none of them are communicable in the sense that they are found in man as they are found in God, we see no reason why we should depart from the old division which has become so familiar in Reformed theology. (Systematic Theology, p. 55–56).'[6]

The focus of the book is the practical and personal outworking of understanding what God is like (his attributes). Again citing the Westminster Catechism, Question 4 asks, "What is God?" The answer is that

> God is a Spirit, infinite, eternal, and unchangeable, in his being, wisdom, power, holiness, justice, goodness, and truth.[7]

---

5. Stone, "Incommunicable Attributes," 1.

6. "Classification of the attributes of God," para. 4.

7. "Westminster Shorter Catechism."

Utilizing God's Attributes—The Example of God's Self-existence

Tozer himself notes,

> All our problems and their solutions are theological. Some knowledge of what kind of God it is that operates the universe is indispensable to a sound philosophy of life and a sane outlook on the world scene.[8]

Solomon, the one to whom God gave wisdom, wrote, "The fear of the LORD is the beginning of wisdom, and knowledge of the Holy One is understanding" (Prov 9:10 NIV).

For each attribute, we should be able to answer the following questions:

• What does it mean?

• How does it impact me?

• How do I live it out, both internally and externally?

Within this introduction, perhaps the best attribute to examine is God's self-existence. First, it is important to define God's self-existence. "Every *effect* must have a *cause*. That is true by definition. But God is not an effect. . . . He has, within Himself, the power of being. He requires no assistance from outside sources to continue to exist. This is what is meant by the idea of *self-existent*."[9]

My bachelor's degree was in philosophy. I've spent much time in the circles of those who enjoy debating such things as the self-existence of God and whether or not it violates logic and reason. However, as Sproul asserts, "The concept of self-existence violates no law of reason, logic, or science. It is a rationally valid notion. By contrast, the concept of self-creation violates the most basic law of reason, logic, and science—the law of noncontradiction. Self-existence is rational; self-creation is irrational."[10]

Furthermore, "The notion of something being self-existent is not only rationally *possible*, it is rationally *necessary*. Again, reason demands that if anything is, then something must have, within itself, the power of being. Otherwise there would be nothing. Unless something existed in itself, nothing could possibly exist at all."[11] How does this impact the way I, as a follower of God, live my life? First, when the attribute of God's self-existence is not lived out, the result is a focus on self. "The natural man is a sinner because and only because he

8. Tozer, *Knowledge of the Holy*, 27.

9. Sproul, *Essential Truths*, 37 (italics original).

10. Sproul, *Essential Truths*, 37–38.

11. Sproul, *Essential Truths*, 38 (italics original).

challenges God's selfhood in relation to his own."[12] So it becomes necessary to embrace God's self-existence if we are to live for others, including living for God's glory. My accepting and trusting in God's self-existence should lead me to the study of his attributes. Internally, I desire to know more and more about this self-existent One. I have a firm and secure foundation upon which to build. My God is there for me. Externally, I treat others with an understanding that reveals that my life is not about me but about the glory of the One who is existent, the Great I AM.

Living Out—The Example of Our Prayer Life

One barometer of how we view God's attributes in our lives is how we pray. If we see God primarily as the One who takes care of our needs, we will treat him like the proverbial cosmic ATM. We will come to him with our needs, wants, and desires. However, if, as we pray, we focus on how a particular attribute of God is relevant to one of those circumstances that weighs heavily, our prayers are transformed. For example, the physical need of a dear one becomes an opportunity for God to be glorified through how he lives out his attribute of omnipotence. This, in turn, gives us the opportunity to share with others who he IS through what he has DONE.

When I pray, I praise God for who he is and thank him for what he's done. These are two sides of the same coin. I know part of God's character (an attribute) through what he does (an action that displays that attribute). And so it is with us. People will know the extent of our becoming like Christ as we live out the various attributes of Christ, thus demonstrating our Christ-like character. Romans 8:29 says, "For those God foreknew he also predestined to be conformed to the image of his Son, that he might be the firstborn among many brothers and sisters." It is God's will that we become more and more like his Son.

This is our number one goal when it comes to cross-cultural ministry—modeling Jesus Christ to those who do not yet know him. A great example of the impact of living this out is found in Daniel 3. This is the familiar story of Shadrach, Meshach, and Abednego defying the decree to fall down and worship the golden image of King Nebuchadnezzar. The king sentenced them to be thrown into a blazing furnace. Their response was a direct statement of what they believed about their God:

> King Nebuchadnezzar, we do not need to defend ourselves before you in this matter. If we are thrown into the blazing furnace,

---

12. Tozer, *Knowledge of the Holy*, 29.

the God we serve is able to deliver us from it, and he will deliver us from Your Majesty's hand. But even if he does not, we want you to know, Your Majesty, that we will not serve your gods or worship the image of gold you have set up. (Dan 3:16–18 NIV)

After the king saw that the three were thrown into the fire without being consumed by it, he called them to himself. The king's exclamation is one that all of us cross-cultural workers dream of hearing:

Praise be to the God of Shadrach, Meshach and Abednego, who has sent his angel and rescued his servants! They trusted in him and defied the king's command and were willing to give up their lives rather than serve or worship any god except their own God. Therefore, I decree that the people of any nation or language who say anything against the God of Shadrach, Meshach and Abednego be cut into pieces and their houses be turned into piles of rubble, for no other god can save in this way. (Dan 3:28–29 NIV)

To God be the glory! God's glory was realized through the living out of God's attributes in the lives of those who knew the reality of his power. Three young men modeled living out God's attributes in cross-cultural ministry.

WHY FOCUS ON CROSS-CULTURAL MINISTRY?

I am being very intentional to use the phrase "cross-cultural ministry" and not "missions." This is for two reasons. First, the word *missions* carries a lot of baggage with it. I personally still like the word, as it communicates the missional aspect of cross-cultural ministry. And, while I believe that all Christians are called to living missionally, I do not believe that all Christians are called to serve God as missionaries. This will be addressed more in chapter 1, when God's sovereignty is discussed in connection with the concept of a call.

The second, and more obvious, reason for leaning more heavily on *cross-cultural ministry* is that the world is all around us, no matter where we are. The mission statement for my intercultural studies major at Lancaster Bible College states, "The intercultural studies major equips servant leaders to be effective cross-cultural communicators, compassionate examples and committed disciple-makers of Jesus Christ." This includes the missionary going from the USA to an unengaged people group in Southeast Asia, as well as the cross-cultural worker serving in downtown Philadelphia.

Living and working cross-culturally presents some unique challenges that can be addressed by living out God's attributes. Being away from home (however you define *home*) means that you're in unfamiliar territory. The support network you have possibly enjoyed is no longer available to you in the same way that it was. Yes, there is social media, but that only partially fills a void. Plus, it can potentially become a distraction from your serving those in your new location. And learning a new culture and language will take a toll on you, both emotionally and physically.

OVERVIEW OF THE BOOK

I wrestled with the framework of this book. I considered ordering the book by prioritizing the attributes of God and how to apply them to various aspects of cross-cultural ministry. In the end, I instead decided to organize the content by the stages of cross-cultural ministry and bring in one of the more relevant attributes of God to each of the following stages of ministry.

- Introduction (Self-existence)
- Part 1: Pre-field
  - Call to Cross-cultural Ministry (Sovereignty)
  - Preparation (Holiness)
  - Between Two Worlds (Omnipresence)
- Part 2: Departure and Entry
  - Saying Good-bye (Faithfulness)
  - Entry—Culture Shock and Culture Stress (Immutability)
  - Adjusting to Team (Grace)
  - Adjusting to the Host Culture (Mercy)
- Part 3: On-field Ministry
  - Connecting with the People (Wisdom)
  - Ministering to the People
    - Ministering to Their Nonspiritual Needs (Love and Justice)
    - Ministering to Their Spiritual Needs (Transcendence)
  - Seeing the Church/Ministry Established (Omnipotence and Immensity)
  - Seeing the Church/Ministry Grow/Multiply (Infinitude)

- Part 4: Return
  - Saying Good-bye to the Ministry Community (Goodness and Immanence)
  - Re-entering the Sending Community (Eternalness)
  - Reporting and Debriefing (Omniscience)
- Conclusion (Knowablity)

With each attribute studied, I identify tangible ways to live it out. Conversely, there are symptoms of not recognizing an attribute's potential application. These, too, will be discussed. In each stage of ministry or circumstance, the question that should be asked is this: What attribute(s) can I see as being relevant to this circumstance, stressor, etc.? As we understand and trust God in his various attributes, we will see our actions flow from that inward formation.[13]

> Pablo Casals was considered to be the preeminent cellist of the first half of the 20th century. When he was still playing his cello in the middle of his tenth decade of life, a young reporter asked him, 'Mr. Casals, you are 95 years old and the greatest cellist that ever lived. Why do you still practice 6 hours a day?' Mr. Casals answered, 'Because I think I'm making progress.'[14]

My desire is that you would see yourself in each of these chapters and contemplate how a better understanding of God will help you to more effectively glorify his name among those he has called you to serve, whether now or in the future.

---

13. Galli, *Great and Terrible Love.*
14. Kasper, *Daily Bread,* December 17, 2014.

PART 1

Pre-field

Chapter 1

Call to Cross-cultural Ministry

Surrendering to God's Sovereignty

"Our God is in the heavens; he does all that he pleases." (Ps 115:3)

"When people ask me how they can know God's will,
I tell them that the best first step is to know God."

—M. DAVID SILLS[1]

I HAVE ALWAYS BEEN a logical man. I lead with my head. In the late 1970s, as I attended a conference sponsored by the US Center for World Missions (a weekend version of the infant Perspectives on the World Christian Movement class), I learned about God's heart for the world. During one of the presentations, a slide on the screen detailed the great need for the gospel to go to China. So few were going to so many who had nearly no opportunity to hear of God's lovingly redemptive plan. The numbers gripped me, and I felt God's leading to be a part of a church-planting effort there. Later, as I had a chance to visit China, my heart caught up to my head. My call was now solidified.

When we lived in China, we often read the *China Daily*, the country's state-run, English-language newspaper. In it we would read how China felt that no other country had the right to impose its will on another sovereign

---

1. Sills, *Missionary Call*, 34.

power. In short, the United States had no right to interfere with matters of China's internal concern. On the other hand, it was not unusual to be asked questions that, at the time, felt too personal—"How old are you?" "How much money do you make?" We often feel the same way about our personal lives or our families when we say (or at least would like to say), "It's none of your business."

GOD'S CALL TO SERVE CROSS-CULTURALLY

In this first chapter revolving around ministering cross-culturally and God's attributes, with the focus on God's sovereignty and man's surrender, I want to challenge you regarding your call to cross-cultural ministry. It may be helpful for you to know that I believe all Christians are called to cross-cultural ministry in one way or another. For some, it will be going to another country or another culture a short distance away from where you currently live. Others will be involved through praying, giving, sending, or welcoming. But all are to be involved in taking the gospel to the world.

On the other hand, I do not believe all Christians are called by God to be missionaries. This gets to be a bit controversial, but that may be a matter of semantics and calling. While all Christians are called to live missionally, not all Christians are called to be Go-ers in the sense of going to live and minister to those in another culture. And if everybody's a missionary, nobody's a missionary. The word *missionary* comes from the Latin root word *missio*, defined as "one who is sent."

Or we could use the word *ambassador*. In 2 Corinthians 5:11–21, a call to the ministry of reconciliation is given. "We are therefore Christ's ambassadors" (20). A country's ambassador is one who is sent with two things: authority and a message. When I would go to the USA Embassy in Bangkok, Thailand, to get more pages in my passport, I would enter the American Services section. There, on the wall, were three pictures—those of the President, the Vice President, and the Secretary of State of the United States of America. The US Ambassador is sent there with the authority and message of the US government, specifically the Secretary of State. Likewise, we take the gospel to another land with God's authority and message.

Herbert Kane writes,

> The Chinese have a proverb: If two men feed a horse, it will lose weight; if two men keep a boat, it will soon leak. What is everybody's job is nobody's job. If every Christian is a missionary, missionary work is bound to suffer. It is correct to say that every

Christian is, or should be, a witness. It is not correct to say that every Christian is a missionary.[2]

Don't get me wrong. We are responsible for living missionally in such a way that we minister to the lost who are living in our neighborhood, wherever that neighborhood is located. And the local church has the responsibility to be a light to those around it. But what happens when there is no local church? Those bearing the light need to take it where it is not being shone. And, as mentioned above, every Christian (and every church) should be involved in this great adventure.

What Constitutes a Call?

What does all of this have to do with God's sovereignty and man's surrender? The key word is *call*. The call of God can seem so nebulous and mysterious. Is it personal and individual? Is it for a lifetime? There are all kinds of questions that are associated with the call of God.

I teach intercultural studies at Lancaster Bible College. In one of my classes, we rehearse the many callings in the Bible. I use a concentric circle diagram to do this, connecting phases of a person's call with each circle, moving from the outside in to the center. The first call from God is the call to salvation. This is a universal call to all people but answered by those who choose to place their trust in Jesus Christ and his finished work on the cross as the payment for their sin debt. The second call, to all believers, is a call to a life of holiness and discipleship. The next circle in is a call to serve God in full-time work. Here, a discussion takes place concerning whether or not the Christian serving in the marketplace (e.g., an accountant) is any less of a servant of God than the missionary serving in a foreign country. The answer, of course, is NO! This is not a question of value but of function:

> I believe that God has called every Christian to the task of international missions. Of course, I do not think we are all to sell the farm and go. . . . Some of us are senders and some are goers. Neither is more important than the other. Neither is possible without the other. The lost cannot be born again without the gospel, and missionaries cannot go preach unless we send them. We all have a role to play in international missions.[3]

For those who are called into full-time Christian (nonmarketplace) ministry, the following distinctions revolve around the specific assignment,

2. Kane, as quoted in Hesse, "Every Believer a Missionary," para. 2.
3. Sills, *Missionary Call*, 30.

task, and context. "Being a missionary begins with a call. You don't choose to be a missionary; you're called to be one. The only choice is whether to obey."[4]

God's sovereignty manifests itself in how he matches need and resource. When my class and I discuss the call of God, I sometimes share the illustration from one of my former professors. I remember his recounting how he would use a world map and have three students each throw a dart on the map. "You've just hit three areas of need. Even if your dart hits an ocean, there's probably a fisherman who needs to know the Lord. The question is not about where the need is—the need is everywhere. The question is, 'Where is God calling you?'" As God has sovereignly equipped each person, he does so for a purpose. How we live out how he's made us to those he has called us to serve will bring him glory as others are gathered to worship him. So the call of God is a matter of our surrendering to his leading. "The biggest hindrance to the missionary task is self. Self that refuses to die. Self that refuses to sacrifice. Self that refuses to give. Self that refuses to go."[5] We need to remind ourselves of how God's sovereignty places us under his lordship. This helps us to listen to his callings, both primary and secondary.

> Our primary calling as followers of Christ is by him, to him, and for him. . . . Our secondary calling, considering who God is as sovereign, is that everyone, everywhere, and in everything should think, speak, live, and act entirely for him. . . . Secondary callings matter, but only because the primary calling matters most.[6]

I have had prospective students come to my office to discuss the intercultural studies major. I can see the passion God has given them in their eyes, and I hear it as they share their stories. It is quite common, during these stories, to have a sentence begin with, "But God . . . ." This is a signal that God, in his sovereignty, is at work in this person's life.

Unfortunately, sometimes that same prospective student has a parent along with them, who follows the child's passionate story with the question, "So what kind of job will my child get with a degree in intercultural studies?" Now I have four daughters, so I understand the concern behind the question. However, I would hope that I would, with each of my daughters, seek God's will for her and not just what the world expects: a well-paying job. For the record, a degree in intercultural studies could very well result in such a job; I keep a file of "Jobs for an intercultural studies graduate" handy

---

4. Hale & Daniels, *On Being a Missionary*, 19.
5. Hale & Daniels, *On Being a Missionary*, 36.
6. Guinness, *Call*, 31 (italics original).

for those times. But that is not the issue here. We have to avoid pushing God's sovereignty in our own lives to the side just to find the "right" job. The right job is the one God leads you to do.

In fact, the result of pursuing a job that provides financial security may actually result in living a life of emotional insecurity and uncertainty. I have met many an adult who shared how he, at a younger age, felt God's leading into ministry. However, "the cares of the world" pushed that leading to the side. Now, looking back, these people wonder whether or not they have missed out on God's best for them.

Some of us struggle with allowing the Lord to be Lord because we tend to seek a basis of trust in our relationships. We see the importance of building trust based upon a history of faithfulness. Unfortunately, we bring that same mentality to our relationship with God. We want him to show us his goodness before we will trust him as the Lord of our lives.

What Does God Use to Call Us?

But what does this look like? How do we bring God's sovereignty, our surrender, and God's call together? What does God use to demonstrate or reveal his sovereignty in our lives? First, ever and always, he uses his word, the Bible. God's will never contradicts his word. But God's word often is used to point us to his specific will. Sometimes it will be a general truth such as the one found in 2 Peter 3:9, where we read that, "The Lord is not slow in keeping his promise, as some understand slowness. Instead he is patient with you, not wanting anyone to perish, but everyone to come to repentance."

And sometimes it will be some of the more overt missionary passages in Scripture. "Declare his glory among the nations, his marvelous deeds among all peoples" (Ps 96:3; see also Mark 16:15 and Matt 28:18–20).

God also uses those in our lives to help us to respond to God's leading, whether it is a matter of confirming, accepting, refining, or otherwise interacting with how we feel the Lord is leading us. We need to draw upon the wise perspective of the God-fearing men and women he has placed around us. Please note that, even from the early stages of exploration, it's important to involve those concerned and not simply inform them. All too often, the hopeful missionaries' families, friends, and churches are simply notified that "God has called" them into ministry without any involvement of those who love God and them. No one person has a monopoly on the Holy Spirit. When somebody plays the "well, God told me to do this" card, it serves as a conversation-killer more than anything else. If a Christian feels that God is speaking to her, she will have others around her that she can draw upon to aid her in discerning what God is saying.

Likewise, God, in his sovereignty, may use circumstances to help guide and direct us in the direction he wants us to go. But how do we discern what is of God and what is not of God? The answer again comes back to our surrendering to him. Even as I was writing this chapter, my wife and I had an appointment with a young woman following the Lord's leading into cross-cultural ministry. It was exciting to hear of how the Lord has brought people into her life along the way. With each new interaction another opportunity to serve arose. And with each new opportunity, she learned more about God, about herself, and about God's future for her. She continues to walk a life of open surrender to her Lord, and he continues to reward her with an unfolding of his direction for her. She is living out Hebrews 11:6: "And without faith it is impossible to please God, because anyone who comes to him must believe that he exists and that he rewards those who earnestly seek him."

And do not underestimate how God has created you. His sovereignty is also revealed in such things as the ways he has formed you, e.g., your physical capabilities and limitations, your personality, and your talents. Additionally, what skills have you been able to develop, e.g., musical, athletic, leadership? What life experiences, both positive and negative, has he been using to further shape you? And who has he brought into your life to impact you, e.g., family, friends, and colleagues? And be careful to consider those that you might normally think of as annoying as possible tools in God's hands. We learn a lot about ourselves when we are under stress. In short, how does the combination of these begin to reveal God's will for you?

Let me give a note about valuing others in this process. We need to be careful to involve others and not just inform them. Many simply inform their family members and church leaders that God has called them to the mission field. It might be a college student coming home during break. Or it could be a more experienced and mature believer who may not see the need to involve others. When we involve others, we honor them and invite them into God's process.

GOD'S CALL—WHY IS IT NONE OF MY BUSINESS?

Remember how I felt about those personal questions I would be asked in China (and other Asian countries)? We often come to a discussion about God's sovereignty with limited understanding of what sovereignty is and what it means. In short, everything is God's business because of his sovereignty. Sovereignty is a combination of superiority and authority. It's about God's being in control of our lives.

As Feinberg points out, "God does his own actions and . . . they are in accord with his choices."[7] The emphasis is always on God's will first before it is on our responses. God's sovereignty insists on our responding in understanding that we are ever and always under his authority. "This notion of divine sovereignty means, of course, that God is the ultimate, final, and complete authority over everything and everyone."[8]

Contemporary culture, perhaps more than in previous eras, struggles with this. "No doctrine is more despised by the natural mind than the truth that God is absolutely sovereign. Human pride loathes the suggestion that God orders everything, controls everything, rules over everything. The carnal mind, burning with enmity against God, abhors the biblical teaching that nothing comes to pass except according to His eternal decrees."[9]

This is why it is essential to establish a strong biblical foundation of what it means for God to be sovereign over his creation. Psalm 115:3 says, "Our God is in the heavens; He does all that He pleases." God does not seek to be understood as much as he desires that we acknowledge that he is our authority.

One of the reasons it is so important to establish God's sovereignty is that we desperately want to exert control over our own lives. To acknowledge that someone else has authority over us and that we are not the masters of our own destiny is a bitter pill to swallow for most. In a small way, when the Chinese asked me how old I was or how much money I made, they were seeking to establish an understanding of our relationship and how to address one another. The question about age directly impacts which title to use, i.e., older or younger brother. Knowing who was higher in age or status led to an expectation of respect.

Tozer encourages us to remember that "God's sovereignty is the attribute by which He rules His entire creation, and to be sovereign God must be all-knowing, all-powerful, and absolutely free."[10] Just as the Chinese labeled me a Foreign Expert and granted me certain privileges accorded those with that title, so we need to understand who God is and then afford him the respect he deserves. When we call him "Lord," it has to mean something.

---

7. Feinberg, *No One Like Him*, 294.
8. Feinberg, *No One Like Him*, 294.
9. MacArthur, "God's Absolute Sovereignty," para. 1.
10. Tozer, *Knowledge of the Holy*, 108.

God's Call—When I Pull Out My Planner

In our attempts to maintain control over our lives we make our lists, schedules, and plans. But as we are reminded in Proverbs 16:9, "In his heart a man plans his course, but the LORD determines his steps."

The story of Joseph presents us with a model of what it means to, at least eventually, concede, confess, and celebrate God's sovereignty. Having been sold into slavery by his brothers, Joseph eventually finds himself as the second in command over Pharaoh's resources during a time of great famine. When his brothers come to realize their brother's power and authority over them, they are filled with fear of how he might treat them. But Joseph is not bitter, for he has come to see how God's sovereign hand has been at work: "But Joseph said to them, 'Don't be afraid. Am I in the place of God? You intended to harm me, but God intended it for good to accomplish what is now being done, the saving of many lives" (Gen 50:19–20).

Christians today often use (and sometimes abuse) this familiar verse: "And we know that in all things God works for the good of those who love him, who have been called according to his purpose" (Rom 8:28). Note the phrase, "according to his purpose." We need to remind ourselves that God's purpose is at the beginning and the end of accepting and celebrating what comes our way. "I make known the end from the beginning, from ancient times, what is still to come. I say: My purpose will stand, and I will do all that I please" (Isa 46:10).

As difficult as it is for us at times, we need to remember that God does not seek our permission to be in control. He *is* in control. It would do us well to not challenge this. "Woe to him who quarrels with his Maker, to him who is but a potsherd among the potsherds on the ground. Does the clay say to the potter, 'What are you making?' Does your work say, 'He has no hands?'" (Isa 45:9–10).

Are we to avoid making plans? No, that is not how we apply an understanding of God's sovereignty. But we make our plans with the knowledge that we are dependent upon God (Jas 4:13–16).

And as we live our lives, we constantly need to remind ourselves of our ultimate purpose—that of bringing glory to God. "In him we were also chosen, having been predestined according to the plan of him who works out everything in conformity with the purpose of his will, in order that we, who were the first to hope in Christ, might be for the praise of his glory" (Eph 1:11–12).

NOT MY WILL BUT HIS?

By now, you have probably caught on to what our response to God's sovereignty should be—surrender. Not a surrender that results in futility but rather a surrender that yields control to the One who is the Alpha and the Omega, the Beginning and the End.

> There is no attribute more comforting to His children than that of God's Sovereignty. Under the most adverse circumstances, in the most severe trials, they believe that Sovereignty has ordained their afflictions, that Sovereignty overrules them, and that Sovereignty will sanctify them all.[11]

Oh, the joy of resting in the knowledge that we are not responsible for all that happens in all of eternity! Some of us carry a weight we were never intended—nor equipped—to carry. We thrive most when we yield all to God. When we cease our striving, we come to understand that we cannot bring about God's glory apart from God's plan and power. We need to let God be God in our lives.

My philosopher friends (from when I majored in Philosophy/Religious Studies for my Bachelor's degree) would, at this time, introduce the discussion of God's sovereignty versus man's free will. How do these meet? Is man truly free to make choices? On the one hand, God's sovereignty in relation to man means that God has the right to do as he desires. But do we have any freedom to affect the outcomes of our lives?

We come to the issue of God's sovereignty and man's free will and realize that the choice we *must* make is to surrender to a sovereign God. To do otherwise would be at best foolish and perhaps even dangerous. On June 4, 1989, the "Tiananmen Incident" (as the Chinese government called it) happened. My family was scheduled to return to the USA for the summer but not until three weeks later. We sought the counsel of one of our older Chinese colleagues. He told us we were fine to wait. Two days later, however, when he came and warned us to get out as soon as possible, we evacuated.

Back in Pennsylvania, I found myself wondering whether or not we should return to our beloved university to continue our English teaching there. When God, through much prayer and many consultations with those we trusted, made it clear that we were to return, some questioned us. At that time, I remember parroting what I had often heard: "the safest place to be is the center of God's will." Today, I would challenge that statement. I do believe that the *best* place to be is the center of God's will, but it may not be the *safest*. While God is committed to meeting all my needs in Christ Jesus,

11. Pink, *Attributes of God*, 31.

that in no way guarantees a safe life—whatever that means. But there is a difference between being in a dangerous place by God's design and being dangerously out of the will of God.

You see, it is God, and only God, who is able to claim sovereignty. Therefore, he is also the only One who can expect us to surrender to his will. Some come to God's sovereignty with fists clenched. Eventually, those fists need to be relaxed and opened up in a demonstration of yielding to God. Whether done reluctantly or expectantly, it is where we need to arrive. The image of the potter and the clay used in Jeremiah points to God's having this level of rule: "'O house of Israel, can I not do with you as this potter does?' declares the LORD. 'Like clay in the hand of the potter, so are you in my hand, O house of Israel'" (Jer 18:6). This understanding helps us to relax in the lordship relationship we have with God.

> To say that God is sovereign is to say that He is supreme over all things, that there is no one above Him, that He is absolute Lord over creation. It is to say that His Lordship over creation means that there is nothing out of His control, nothing that God hasn't foreseen and planned . . . . God's sovereignty logically implies His absolute freedom to do all that He wills to do.[12]

When we lose sight of this, we again close our hands in an attempt to assume control over our lives. We follow the world's pattern by demanding our rights. Part of the reason for our lack of trust in how God will exercise his sovereign control is that we fail to recognize that it is paired with his other attributes, including his goodness. When this happens, we pull back and focus on our rights. But we don't have any rights—at least, not apart from God's sovereign will (Col 1:16–17).

Regarding God's sovereignty and the cross (salvation), "What does all this mean to you and me? It means that if you walk out of church contrary to the will and way of God, God does not will that you should do it, but He wills that you should be free to do it. And when you freely choose to walk against the way of God, you choose freely to go on the road to perdition."[13] Similarly, when God reveals his will/call for our lives, we have the freedom to choose to obey and follow his leading. But we also have the freedom to not follow his leading. The loss will be ours, not God's. It is better to surrender—for our sake and for God's glory.

Are you wondering what God's future (long-term or short-term) for you might be? If so, here are some steps that you can be taking right now to position yourself well to hear from him and joyfully surrender to his will:

12. Tozer, *Attributes of God*, 2:144.

13. Tozer and Fessenden, *Attributes of God*, 2:160.

1. Seek God's sovereign leading as you read the Bible.

2. Seek confirmation from those God has in your life. Don't easily dismiss a comment from someone you trust who is walking closely with God.

3. Believe God for the next step, whatever it might be.

4. Take those next steps, one at a time.

   ◆ Some examples of next steps

   > Discuss your thoughts and feelings with your family

   > Talk with those at your church

   > Contact an organization, e.g., a sending agency

   > Research a people group (see Operation World or Joshua Project)

   > Take the Perspectives on the World Christian Movement (www.Perspectives.org) course

As you grow in your appreciation of God's sovereignty, be intentional about growing in your daily surrender to God. Part of that is asking him to show you his hand at work in the lives and circumstances he brings into your life. Again, don't dismiss something too quickly or casually. And remember to trust the Holy Spirit in you as well as in those around you.

GOD'S SOVEREIGNTY—WILL I SURRENDER?

In the end (of the beginning), it comes down to this one question: Are you willing to surrender your life, in its entirety as well as in the small details, to the Sovereign Lord? To the extent that you believe him to be above all and over all, including yourself, you will gladly—and perhaps with a measure of healthy fear—sing the song

> All to Jesus I surrender, All to Him I freely give;
> I will ever love and trust Him, In His presence daily live.
> All to Jesus I surrender, Humbly at His feet I bow,
> Worldly pleasures all forsaken; Take me, Jesus, take me now.
> All to Jesus I surrender, Lord, I give myself to Thee;
> Fill me with Thy love and power, Let Thy blessing fall on me.
> All to Jesus I surrender, Now I feel the sacred flame.
> Oh, the joy of full salvation! Glory, glory to His name!
> I surrender all, I surrender all.
> All to Thee, my blessed Savior, I surrender all.[14]

14. http://www.lyricsondemand.com/miscellaneouslyrics/christianlyrics/

It was in a freezing cold classroom in Harbin, Heilongjiang Province—in northeast China—when God confirmed my call to China. I was on a survey trip to several cities in China, asking God if this was, indeed, what he had for me. I remember sitting in a classroom with about twenty college students. It was English Corner time, a time for them to practice their spoken English. I told them that they could ask me any question they wanted to ask. If I felt it was too personal, I would tell them, but I would attempt to answer as many as I could. As the afternoon wore on, I found myself being drawn to them and their minds and hearts. When I was asked how I could believe in both science and God, I felt a spark within me. I almost chuckled at how God was drawing together my background in philosophy and my heart for the Chinese. I left that room feeling more alive than I had for quite some time. This is what God had created me to do!

My prayer for you is that you would experience the deep satisfaction of knowing the Sovereign Lord and the joy of surrendering your will to him.

QUESTIONS

1. How has God shown himself to be sovereign in your life? Be specific.

2. What makes it difficult for you to personally surrender to God?

3. As best you understand it right now, what do you believe to be God's call for you?

4. Whom would you trust to ask for prayer about this? Make a list and then follow up by asking for prayer from each.

alltojesusisurrenderlyrics.html.

Chapter 2

Preparing for Cross-cultural Ministry

Holiness That Leads to Discipline

"Be holy because I am holy." (1 Pet 1:16)

"Holy is the way God is. To be holy He does not conform to a standard. He is that standard."

—A. W. Tozer[1]

I'M NOT A BUTCHER, but I do love my meat. In fact, every fall semester, my wife and I host Meat Night for the male intercultural studies majors at Lancaster Bible College. (The ladies get a special dessert night of their own later on.) When it comes to meat, especially beef steak, three important factors are involved: the cut of meat, the seasoning/marinating of that meat, and the actual grilling. I love to grill, and I know that it's important to know how to choose and prepare the meat before putting it on the grill.

And so it is with our preparation for cross-cultural ministry. God knows that we need to be set apart (the choosing or call) and prepared (seasoned) for service. In this chapter, as we focus on preparation for ministry, I want to focus on God's attribute of holiness and our being seasoned for ministry.

1. Tozer, *Knowledge of the Holy*, 105.

PATIENCE IN PREPARATION—"BUT WE JUST WANT TO GO!"

My wife Carol and I got married soon after we graduated from university. We knew that God had called us into ministry in China, but we were unsure of how to connect the dots to get there. We didn't have a sending church, and we were ignorant of the role of the sending agency.

Fortunately, God led us to a solid Bible-believing, missions-oriented church. When we involved the pastor, he brought us to a friend of his, Ted Fletcher—the founder of what is now Pioneers, International. We found a strong fit with Pioneers and soon found ourselves going through the process to become missionary appointees. This began a journey of preparation for us.

The partnership between our strong sending church, a great sending agency, and ourselves played itself out as perfectly as we could have hoped. We invested deeply into the church, and the church reciprocated by supporting us for nearly thirty years! And the church/agency relationship grew over the years. We felt loved and cared for by both church and agency.

Of course, even in the early stages of this partnership, there were times of frustration. "We just want to go!" "Why do we have to do all this other stuff first?" For us, this revolved around two requirements that were given to us. First, even though we had been involved in ministry on the university campus, we were asked to get formal Bible training. So we went to a Bible college in Tennessee (one of our first cross-cultural experiences). We did a year of Bible and missions classes before returning to Pennsylvania to accomplish the second requirement, my getting a Master's degree in Teaching English as a Second Language (TESL).

During this time, we continued to grow relationships in and out of our sending church. God also used this time to develop us as individuals and as a couple. We were learning the importance of becoming who God wanted us to be before doing what he intended for us to do. We needed to grow in our personal holiness and obedience. We also needed to learn that obedience was not an end in itself.

> But when we truly understand that God justifies us out of loving divine grace, and not because of our holiness or our obedience to the law, this law that previously seemed bitter turns sweet, for now the commandment becomes a promise.[2]

I'm sure much more happened during this time of which I'm not even aware. In short, God was continuing to prepare us for the work that he had called us to do.

2. González, *Knowing Our Faith*, 77.

BEGINNING OF PREPARATION—
SET APART FOR A PURPOSE

The Greek word *hagios* is most often translated as "holy," "set apart," or "sacred." The idea is that of a piece of meat cut apart with an intended purpose, much like the meats I look forward to grilling for Meat Night. After choosing the cut of meat, the customer may ask the butcher to choose to not only cut the chosen piece but to also trim some of the fat. All of this is done before taking the chosen piece and seasoning or marinating it in preparation for cooking. In Jesus' priestly prayer (John 17:13–19), he prays for us to be sanctified.

> Therefore, I urge you, brothers, in view of God's mercy to offer your bodies as living sacrifices, holy and pleasing to God—this is your spiritual act of worship. (Rom 12:1)

We see in Scripture that there is a setting apart with the desire for a subsequent behavior change. And just as a piece of meat is cut apart from the larger piece for a purpose, it also needs to be further prepared for its intended purpose. It may need to be pounded (yikes!), trimmed, and seasoned or marinated. This time of preparation is essential. Likewise, the time of preparation for the cross-cultural worker cannot be skipped.

> Therefore, prepare your minds for action; be self-controlled; set your hope fully on the grace to be given you when Jesus Christ is revealed. As obedient children, do not conform to the evil desires you had when you lived in ignorance. But just as he who called you is holy, so be holy in all you do; for it is written: "Be holy, because I am holy." (1 Pet 1:13–16)

Yes, God is holy. "Holy is the way God is. To be holy He does not conform to a standard. He is that standard."[3] Jesus is often referred to as "the Holy One of God." He will be worshipped for his holiness (Rev. 4:8; 15:4). We need to make sure that we do not treat God too casually. He is a *holy* God that demands that we, too, be holy. "Be ye holy, for I am holy." (1 Pet 1:13–16) And it's easy to see the connection between holiness (being) and obedience (doing).

The purpose of our seeking to be holy is to glorify and reflect God's holiness. "Until we have seen ourselves as God sees us, we are not likely to be much disturbed over conditions around us as long as they not get so far out of hand as to threaten our comfortable way of life. We have learned to

---

3. Tozer, *Knowledge of the Holy*, 105.

live with unholiness."[4] This is unacceptable to God. "Because God is holy He hates all sin."[5] This hatred for sin is modeled to us in how he acts. "God's holiness is manifested in His works. 'The Lord is righteous in all His ways, and holy in all His works' (Ps. 145:17)"[6] Therefore, our works should reflect the holiness we seek to radiate.

Just as Isaiah's vision of God's holiness ("Woe to me, for I am undone.") is linked to his call to service ("Here am I. Send me," Isa 6:4–9), so should our response to God's holiness and sovereignty be that of surrender and dedication. This is a call to a life of holiness and obedience.

Holiness—The Easy Way or the Hard Way

It is clear from the above discussion that holiness is a communicable attribute of God. It is impossible for us to truly be holy in and of ourselves. But we can, by God's grace and the power of the Holy Spirit, grow in holiness. A significant part of our preparation is developing the skills to do just this—grow in holiness.

All believers are called to live holy lives that glorify God. Holiness refers to the absence of flaws. When the Israelites went to choose a lamb for sacrifice, they were to choose one without blemish. And so it was with our Savior, the Lamb of God, who came to take away the sin of the world (John 1:29). A danger for many of us believers is that we think we must somehow manufacture this holiness. In essence, we're happy to exchange our works-based attempts at salvation for God's grace; however, we again take it upon ourselves and attempt to live out a works-based sanctification. Paul rebukes the Galatians for this when he writes,

> You foolish Galatians! Who has bewitched you? Before your very eyes Jesus Christ was clearly portrayed as crucified. I would like to learn just one thing from you; Did you receive the Spirit by observing the law or by believing what you heard? Are you so foolish? After beginning with the Spirit are you now trying to attain your goal by human effort? Have you suffered so much for nothing—if it really was for nothing? Does God give you his Spirit and work miracles among you because you observe the law, or because you believe what you heard? (3:1–5)

4. Tozer, *Knowledge of the Holy*, 103.
5. Pink, *Attributes of God*, 42
6. Pink, *Attributes of God*, 41.

The authors of *TrueFaced: Trust God with Who You Really Are* (more recently, *The Cure*) do an excellent job of drawing this distinction. They utilize Robert Frost's poem, "The Road Not Taken," as a metaphor of two paths of following God. The more-traveled path leads to the room of good intentions, a room where the Christian works to become holy and pleasing to God. The problem here is that the resulting effort ends up as a sin management program, a never-ending endeavor. Going on to the less-traveled path, the Christian comes to the room of grace. Here, the Christian is encouraged to simply live out who he/she is in Christ—in short, *be* who he/she is in Christ. Sin, in this room, is not a barrier between the Christian and God but rather something that is worked on together *with* Christ. Living out our relationship with Christ makes it easier to live out a life of holiness and obedience.

WHY HOLY PREPARATION?— ATTRITION NUMBERS ARE UP

I remember often hearing Ted Fletcher say, "All the easy places are reached. It's time to go to the hard places." But the truth of today's world is that more and more of the world is becoming hard to reach. Attrition numbers confirm this, as more and more missionaries are leaving the field earlier and earlier.

Elliot Stephens's recent research on retention and onboarding reveals just how imperative it is to do a better job of preparing for service, both before going to the field and after arriving on the field:

> So 50% of agencies are not receiving their new arrivals in a way that helps them stay and thrive. And agencies are losing 50% of their workers by year five. Engage research also discovered that only 38% of missionaries felt their agency was able to equip those struggling for effectiveness in ministry. Some, if not most, of those struggling were probably among the first termers since attrition rates were highest during the first five years on the field.[7]

His research helps to highlight broad areas of concern:

> Our research suggested three areas of equipping necessary for shaping content for the onboarding process. First, clinging fiercely to God because of His pursuit of us, which I'll call spiritual vitality. Second, learning how to build healthy relationships in all directions, which is relational maturity. Third, learning

---

7. Stephens, "Retention and Onboarding," 15–16.

how to do effective ministry in context among the unreached, or ministry effectivity.[8]

As we talk about being set apart for a purpose—service to the Living God—it makes sense that knowing him should be priority one in preparation:

> The highest factor discovered in our research for retention was a deep pursuit of God with a rich understanding of His character. Spiritual disciplines are critical, but even more critical are the motives behind those disciplines and the goal for the time spent with God.[9]

Without this deep relationship with God, missionaries will be susceptible to Satan's original question: "Did God really say . . . ?" (Gen 3:1). It makes sense that knowing God will lead to a proper view of him, which leads to a proper view of ourselves:

> This awareness of the character of God produces the highest character trait for retention in the lives of missionaries, which is a posture of heart in humility and teachability. Some teams and bases look for teachability as the most important character quality when screening for new workers. Field leaders have rejected well-trained candidates because of their lack of teachability.[10]

Some attrition is preventable, and some isn't, but one thing is clear: we have to do a better job of being prepared on the spiritual and moral levels. Missionary appointees, as well as those already in the field, need to be willing to periodically step back and evaluate how they are doing in heart issues.

Early on in our time in Shanghai, Carol and I were taken to an open-air antique market. One of my treasured possessions today is a small wooden object bought at that market. It is a version of a baker's mold. In the mold is the four-word idiom that roughly translates into "now fit to serve." It was used as a type of diploma, awarded to those who successfully completed preparation to serve on the emperor's court. I often bring it into my class to talk about the importance of preparing to serve the King. It reminds me of all the preparation Esther went through in preparation of becoming the queen. Keep in mind that going through the preparation does not guarantee actually going to the field, but it does enhance the likelihood of both going and sustaining through difficult times.

8. Stephens, "Retention and Onboarding," 17.

9. Stephens, "Retention and Onboarding," 17.

10. Stephens, "Retention and Onboarding," 17.

As Dr. Peter Teague, former president of Lancaster Bible College, has often said (related to why one should consider coming to LBC) "If you're going to chop wood, we'll sharpen your axe." Such is the value of solid preparation.

GOD HATES SIN! "OUR GOD IS A CONSUMING FIRE" (HEB 12:29)

God chose us to serve him. But he also wants us to be fit for service. This is not simply a sin-management program. However, it does entail our addressing sin in our life so that we can best be ready to accomplish his purposes in our lives. For each of us, this may look different. The sin that trips me up may not be the same sin that trips you up.

Having said that, one area in which we need to seek to become holy is in the area of purity. In this age when pornography is so rampant, the missionary field is not unaffected. We need to practice holiness in our thought life and how we live in relationship with one another. The motivation to do this will come both externally (possible fear of being caught) and internally (the desire to glorify God). Many external helps for how one is accountable exist and should be utilized. For example, there are many software programs that will monitor internet use. This is a good step to providing a safety net for those more susceptible to online pornography.

We have some dear friends who have served in Thailand for nearly twenty years. Before going to the field, they knew that they had to work on their marriage and personal struggles—and a desire to be holy like Christ. He had to address sexual addiction, pornography, and morality issues. We all knew that serving in Southeast Asia presents spiritual warfare in these areas. Once a missionary gets to the field, he is bombarded with instability due to a lack of security, safety, resources, and previously relied-upon people. It becomes all the more important to be disciplined, to live a holy life, to enter the battle, with possibly just God and you (without the familiar support structure from home). One must know how to live in holiness and how to walk in his power.

Whether it's pornography or some other sin, those who want to serve the King cross-culturally must invest in ruthless preparation. Pre-field training needs to address this area as well as the seemingly more practical areas of preparation. Building a life of discipline is similar to building a trellis upon which a grape vine can be shaped. A trellis not only gives support to the grapevine, it also gives direction for growth. In our lives, certain structures need to be created and cultivated under the guidance of the Holy Spirit and those who love both God and the missionary appointee. This is where spiritual disciplines, or a rule of life, can be helpful.

I remember attending our candidate orientation program, thinking we were ready to leave. As mentioned earlier, we had to take two more years for formal Bible/missions training and studying for my MA TESL degree. We wanted to leave but became thankful for the preparation. We were so much better prepared for teaching in China and staying longer. As those preparing to be tentmakers (those who have an established profession where they serve), we were encouraged to be ready to "make good tents." We became disciplined to follow suggestions from leadership and disciplined to fulfill requirements.

Those serving anywhere must learn to feed themselves spiritually, to interact with God's holiness, and to be holy. It can be a desert out on the field, and it can suck the life out of you.

Another area of concern can be discretionary time. For many, there is no time clock to punch. Learning the disciplines of feeding self, planning, and strategic planning is essential. Some struggle with getting to the field and not having the structure of a 9–5 job and other fixed portions of their daily and weekly schedule. When culture shock hits, it's tempting to retreat into self and unintentionally waste hours upon hours. It becomes imperative that habits be developed that can be utilized in such times *before* one goes out into the field.

The first call of the believer is a call to holiness and obedience. Surrendering to God allows him to season us for his service. This results in something wonderful—a life devoted to God and a fragrant aroma to those around the obedient Christian. And like the meat we served at Meat Nights, it leaves a pleasant taste to those who benefit from it. I remember one Meat Night in particular. Jon, a basketball player, took full advantage of the well-prepared and cooked meat. After several helpings, he got up from the table, lay down on the floor and said, "It is well with my soul." All of our hard work in choosing and preparing the meat was realized in Jon's deep sense of satisfaction. May those around you see one who has been well prepared by God and feel blessed by your presence.

QUESTIONS

1. How would you assess your ability to live a disciplined/holy life at this time?

2. Can you identify one or more areas that need to be pruned by God?

3. What support structures do you need to develop?

4. What specific steps can you take over the next month? Who will you enlist to hold you accountable?

Chapter 3

Living in Two Worlds

God's Omnipresence That Yields Patience

"God did this so that they would seek Him and perhaps reach out for Him and find Him, though He is not far from any one of us. 'For in Him we live and move and have our being'" (Acts 17:27–28).

"Every dreamer knows that it is possible to be homesick for a place you've never been to, perhaps more homesick than for familiar ground."

—JUDITH THURMAN[1]

IN MY CULTURAL ANTHROPOLOGY class, we discuss rites of passage that exist in almost every culture. For example, most cultures have some way of marking birth, adulthood, marriage, and death. Between stages of life, there is a period of time referred to as liminality. It is a time when you are not fully out of the previous stage and not yet in the new stage. One example would be the engagement period for a couple getting ready to get married. These periods of liminality come with a mixture of expectations, and, often, confusion.

So it sometimes is with getting ready to go to the mission field. At times, it seems as though departure will never come. And sometimes, it

---

1. Judith Thurman, desk calendar—1000 places to visit before you die, 2014.

feels as though you have one foot on the boat and one on the dock. It can be frustrating living in between two worlds. The thing is, we are not meant to live between two worlds. We are called to live in today.

For Carol and me, the liminal state of getting ready to go and actually going happened quickly. I was ten months into my one-year accelerated Master's degree studies when I received a contract in the mail. It was from a large university in China. I had no idea how they had gotten my name. But then I found out that a friend of mine, a university professor, had been in China that past summer with a short-term team. As he was about to leave, another university in the same city contacted the university where his team had served and asked if there were any teachers available. My friend sent them my resume, and I soon received a contract in the mail. That was the first I had heard about any of this. So I graduated in December, and we flew to China a month later.

This is not normally how it goes. For most, there are times of wondering how long the wait will be or if departure will ever happen. It is during these stretches that it helps to have the big picture in mind and how God is present throughout. He never leaves us nor forsakes us (Matt 28:20). It is this promise, along with others, upon which we need to lean in times of liminality.

WHAT'S THE RUSH TO LEAVE?

It helps to examine our own thoughts and emotions when we get frustrated with not being there (wherever there is) yet. Is it simply that we feel that the others over there can't get by without us? Or that we won't really be doing God's work until we get there? Or that our value is somehow tied to being there and no longer here? These and other possible questions should be examined, for each reveals something about our view of God or of ourselves. We must be careful not to put on ourselves an expectation that God doesn't have.

Being impatient reveals a lack of recognizing God's presence in our current situation. We can miss out on what God is doing during these liminal states. When Carol and I were in the stage of preparing to go, we talked with our sending church pastor about how we could be more involved at the church. He knew that we had been active in campus outreach when we were in college, so he asked if we could help launch a ministry focused on discipleship and evangelism. We jumped in and watched the Lord work in the lives of many at the church. It was a blessed time of investing in the church. At the same time, many relationships were developed, relationships that have lasted more than thirty years.

I am convinced that a lot of our success on the mission field was in large measure the result of the prayers of the saints we got to know during that in-between stage. And the impact of that time will only be known on the other side of eternity. I shudder to think of what we would have missed out on if we would have allowed ourselves to be so focused on going that we neglected to live in the present at that time. On top of that, Carol and I learned many lessons of how to impart knowledge in community and how to trust God with the results.

Likewise, during our last twelve years on the mission field, I was the Area Leader for Mainland Southeast Asia. In short, I was a team leader to many team leaders. When our area began to explode with personnel, we realized that we needed to grow a team around us to help us to care for our field workers. We were pleasantly amazed when Joe and Ann (not their real names), longtime friends from our sending church, shared with us that they felt that God was calling them to join us. We couldn't wait for them to come and help us out, along with the others God subsequently called to work with us. But Joe and Ann had to go through their own preparation, including Joe's taking some Bible classes required by the sending agency. That was difficult, at times, for Joe. And, if I'm being honest, it was difficult for me, too! I wanted them there with us as soon as possible. But we all also recognized the value of their coming to the field well prepared.

As I write the above paragraph, it is with a deep sense of gratitude for all that God did through Joe and Ann on the field for nearly twenty years. They are coming over for dinner this evening, and I'm looking forward to hearing how God has been present even as they conclude their overseas service.

One of the dangers of being frustrated about not yet being *there* is that we do not fully live in the present. God still has us *here* for a reason, and we don't want to miss it. While anticipation is great, it could also rob us of present blessings—blessings to give and to receive. Long before mindfulness became a popular teaching, "Be here now" bumper stickers could be seen on cars. The concept is still the same. We need to not focus so much on the past and future as on the present. That doesn't mean that we give no thought to those nonpresent times. It just means that God has us in this time and with a purpose for it. So the challenge becomes one of growing in anticipation without compromising being present.

GOD IS HERE, NEAR

When we are in those times of frustration, it is helpful to remember God's omnipresence. He is here with us and always will be. But we don't always feel God's presence. Part of the challenge is that we talk about God in spatial language (including time), but he is not limited in these ways. *Dr. Who* fans will recognize the concept of being "bigger on the inside." God is like this—he is much bigger than we can even imagine.

We need to remember the heart of the concept of presence. It is nearness, living close by. Abiding with God should be a present experience, not only something we look back at or forward to. As we think about this, we should be drawn to John 15, where Jesus talks about abiding. Using the imagery of a branch's abiding in the vine, we are encouraged to abide in (remain with, dwell with, tabernacle with, live in close relationship to) Christ. This is not a matter of proximity but of connection.

When we do not feel God's nearness, it is not because he has left us or wandered away—it is we who have moved away. When God asked Adam, "Where are you?" (Gen 3:9), it was so Adam could identify the distance he had attempted to put between himself and God. How often do we do the same thing and then ask God why he has left us?

In his prayer of dedication of the temple, Solomon recognized God's nearness and farness:

> But will God really dwell on earth? The heavens, even the highest heaven, cannot contain You. How much less this temple I have built! Yet give attention to your servant's prayer and his plea for mercy, O LORD my God. Hear the cry and the prayer that your servant is praying in Your presence this day. May Your eyes be open toward this temple night and day, this place of which You said, "My Name shall be there," so that You will hear the prayer Your servant prays toward this place. Hear the supplication of Your servant and of Your people Israel when they pray toward this place. Hear from heaven, Your dwelling place, and when you hear, forgive. (1 Kgs 8:27–30)

Solomon recognizes God's being both far off ("from heaven") and his nearness ("in Your presence this day"). Holding these two in balance is essential for us. We must never forget that God is God. He is not just a nice uncle upon whose lap we can climb and ask for a piece of candy. Likewise, we must remember that God is, indeed, near to us and desires that we enjoy close fellowship with him.

God's Omnipresence in Two Dimensions

God's being with us always has two dimensions to it. First, he is always with us *wherever* we are. There is nowhere we can go that he is not there with us. But, secondly, it also means that he is always with us *whenever* we are. In other words, he is with us where we are now. But he is also going ahead of us before we get there. Not only that, he remains behind us when we leave.

This last point is especially comforting as we contemplate leaving loved ones behind. Isn't it nice to know that the God that goes before you also remains behind you? He will be there with those you leave. You don't have to carry that burden with you. For many, this will be trusting God to look after aging parents, younger siblings, or nieces and nephews. Or it may be that you're concerned about unsaved family or friends who won't have your presence to help them along their faith journey. Or it might be a lack of confidence that the ministry you're in right now will continue to thrive after you've left. But God will still be there! And not only will he still be there, he's also already been orchestrating what he plans to do after you've left. Sometimes we have to wrestle with our being dispensable—the thought that we might not be as essential as we think.

God's omnipresence gives us comfort. "God is equally near to all parts of His universe."[2] He's not like the circus plate-spinner who must frantically move from one stick to another to keep the many plates spinning up high. No, God is at all places at all times. As you think about leaving all things familiar for many things that are new and, sometimes, not so exciting, remember that God goes with you each step of the way.

God is everywhere at all times. Obviously, this is one of God's incommunicable attributes, since we can be only at one place at a time. When preparing to serve God cross-culturally, it's tempting to want to get there as soon as possible.

We are aliens in a strange land. Our homesickness for heaven sometimes also is felt for the place where he wants us to pour out our lives for those he loves. Melanie's (not her real name) getting ready to serve in the Middle East. Her pastor encouraged her in this stage that was taking longer than anticipated. However, he also made it clear that he would not simply be a cheerleader. He wanted to exhort her to embrace this phase of ministry and to see God's presence in it. He emphasized that God is at work in the here and now of her ministry. So she should not risk missing what God is doing now by focusing too much on what he will have her do in the future.

---

2. Tozer, *Knowledge of the Holy,* 119.

This is wisdom from God. And what a blessing to have a pastor with an understanding of the bigger picture. May God help you to find those who love both God and you and are willing to help you walk through what can sometimes be times of impatience and frustration.

God is here with you now, ever, and always.

QUESTIONS

1. How are you doing with your contentment with regards to where you are right now? Can you identify where you might be discontent?

2. Do you have one or more people who love God and you? How can you invite them to walk alongside of you during this phase of preparation?

3. How can you develop your anticipation without jeopardizing being present where you are now? Are there any ways for you to more deeply connect with your sending church and loved ones?

4. Who will you find it most difficult to leave behind? What can you do now to ease that stress? What do you need to trust God to do in their lives?

PART 2

Departure and Entry

Chapter 4

Departure

God's Faithfulness in the Good-byes

"The One who calls you is faithful, and He will do it." (1 Thess 5:24)

"Upon God's faithfulness rests our whole hope of future blessedness."

—A. W. TOZER[1]

WE WERE READY TO go. Plane tickets had been bought, and it was soon time to leave. Finally. But then reality set in. We had to say good-bye. Our sending church scheduled our commissioning service, a time for them to lay hands on us in prayer and to send us on our way.

I remember that evening so vividly. Ted Fletcher, the founder of Pioneers, made the trip to be a part of the commissioning. He had walked with us through the process of our being appointed and prepared. When he spoke to the congregation, he gushed over us and shared the story of "The Law of Small Potatoes." Legend has it that Chinese farmers once decided to enjoy the large potatoes they harvested and to plant the remaining smaller potatoes. The result was, after just a few planting seasons, the harvest was of marble-sized potatoes. The farmers learned that, in order to get large potatoes, they had to sacrificially plant large potatoes.

---

1. Tozer, *Knowledge of the Holy*, 81.

His point in sharing this story was that our church was, in his eyes, sacrificially "planting" some large potatoes (us!) in the mission field. As such, the church was to be commended. However, it also had a responsibility to care for their investment by being committed to prayer on our behalf.

Carol and I felt tremendous support from both the sending agency and the sending church as we prepared to leave. Nonetheless, we soon realized the full weight of saying good-bye to so many loved ones, both family and friends.

Sometimes, departure can feel like a finish line. But it is really just another starting point. Working through the arduous process of raising support and all of the other pre-field requirements, it is sometimes hard to believe that departure will ever come. But God is faithful, and he knows when it's best for you to leave. He has been faithful in preparing you for this time.

IDENTIFYING OUR FEARS WHEN PREPARING TO DEPART

Tozer writes, "Upon God's faithfulness rests our whole hope of future blessedness."[2] Indeed, without God's faithfulness, we would have no hope of accomplishing what we've prepared to do.

It helps to be honest with ourselves and to, among other things, identify the fears we may be feeling as we prepare to launch. These fears might include concern for what we are leaving behind or for where we are going. Or it might even include a fear of the actual trip from here to there.

As mentioned in the previous chapter, we may have concerns regarding those that we are leaving behind. We might be concerned for those who have physical issues. Or we may be nervous about those who have not come to faith in Christ yet. Who will care for them? Likewise, what about the ministry we have worked so hard on as we have prepared to leave? Who will take my place?

As we were planning to leave, all four of our parents gave us their blessing. This was huge for us. We know that this is not always the case for those leaving. It is hard to leave when parents or other loved ones make it more difficult. And I'm not just talking about unsaved parents who may not understand. I remember one mother at our church saying something close to the following: "I want the Lord to send missionaries, but I don't want him to send my children. I will not let them go if he does." To be honest, I was stunned when I heard this. I can only imagine how hard it was for her son and his family when the Lord did, in fact, call them to serve overseas.

2. Tozer, *Knowledge of the Holy*, 81.

On the other hand, earlier this year, we were on the other side of the security gate. It was time to send our eldest daughter and her family to Southeast Asia to begin their cross-cultural ministry. As tears streamed down our faces, we rested in God's ability to watch over them in our absence.

For many who go to the field, they will have spent considerable time with the sending church. For us, it was developing the evangelism/discipleship ministry. What happens to a ministry like this when we leave? Two plans need to be in place. The first is to, as early as possible, develop a transition plan for leadership and responsibility. The second is to cultivate trust in God's ability to watch over that transition after you leave. We saw this happen with Bob's being willing to take over the leadership of the ministry and doing it with excellence. Bob has demonstrated faithfulness in service at the sending church for more than thirty-five years, including the evangelism/discipleship ministry and the missions leadership team. Oh, how thankful we are for Bob and his faithfully serving our faithful God!

EVEN IN DEPARTURE, HE IS FAITHFUL

It is in times of launching that we lean heavily on God's faithfulness. "Upon God's faithfulness rests our whole hope of future blessedness. Only as He is faithful will His covenants stand and His promises be honored. Only as we have complete assurance that He is faithful may we live in peace and look forward with assurance to the life to come."[3]

Many gospel presentations have included illustrations about the difference between the amount of one's faith and the object of one's faith. Typically, the emphasis is placed on the priority of the object of faith. For example, the amount of an ice skater's faith is less important than the object of her faith: the thickness of the ice upon the lake. She could have all the faith in the world, but if the ice is only 1–2 inches thick, she's going through it. On the other hand, having only a little bit of faith in the one-foot-thick ice will be rewarded. This, in turn, will result in increased faith. And so it is with God. He is a faithful object of our faith (Deut 7:9; Lam 3:22–23).

God's faithfulness is sure. And the more we test it, the more we will trust it. Time is often linked to faithfulness, along with patience. Our confidence is not in the *when* but in the *certainty* of God's doing what he promised he would do. Our view of timing is naturally skewed, since we don't have God's perspective on the big picture. His faithfulness is revealed in many ways, including his timing:

3. Tozer, *Knowledge of the Holy*, 81.

> But when the set time had fully come, God sent His Son, born
> of a woman, born under the law, to redeem those under the law,
> that we might receive adoption to sonship. (Gal 4:4–5)

It is also seen in God's being faithful in how he forgives. "If we confess our sins, He is faithful and just and will forgive us our sins and purify us from all unrighteousness" (1 John 1:9).

We need to *wait with hope*. Hope has one eye on the past and one on the future. Especially at times of transition, as with the approaching departure, we need to see how God is true to himself in the past and present as we trust him for the future.

> So then, those who suffer according to God's will should commit
> themselves to their faithful Creator and continue to do good.
> (1 Pet 4:19)

> The One who calls you is faithful, and He will do it. (1 Thess 5:24)

God's faithfulness makes him both consistent and predictable when it comes to his character. This, in turn, helps us to trust in his faithfulness. God's faithfulness also helps us to be faithful to him:

> No temptation has overtaken you except what is common to
> mankind. And God is faithful; He will not let you be tempted
> beyond what you can bear. But when you are tempted, He will
> also provide a way out so that you can endure it. (1 Cor 10:13)

In the first verse and chorus of "Great is Thy faithfulness," we sing

> Great is Thy faithfulness
> O God my Father
> There is no shadow of turning with Thee
> Thou changest not
> Thy compassions they fail not
> As Thou hast been
> Thou forever will be
>
> Great is Thy faithfulness
> Great is Thy faithfulness
> Morning by morning new mercies I see
> And all I have needed Thy had hath provided
> Great is Thy faithfulness
> Lord unto me

As seen in this hymn and many of the verses already quoted, we are reminded that God's attributes work in concert with each other.

> God's attributes are not isolated traits of His character but facets of His unitary being. They are not things-in-themselves; they are, rather, thoughts by which we think of God, aspects of a perfect whole, names given to whatever we know to be true of the Godhead. To have a correct understanding of the attributes it is necessary that we see them all as one . . . All of God's acts are consistent with all of His attributes.[4]

It is not unusual for someone to emphasize one of God's attributes without considering how it interacts with one or more of his other attributes. For example, some today are attempting to justify loving relationships that are against Scripture by saying that God is loving and would look favorably on any loving relationship. However, that fails to recognize that the God of love is also a God of justice and holiness. And so it goes for us. We need to recognize that God cannot cease to be all that he is. His faithfulness, for example, pervades all of his actions:

> Faithfulness is that in God which guarantees that He will never be or act inconsistent with Himself.[5]

> In all His relations with His people God is faithful. He may be safely relied upon. No one ever yet really trusted Him in vain. We find this precious truth expressed almost everywhere in the Scriptures, for His people need to know that faithfulness is an essential part of the Divine character. This is the basis of our confidence in Him. But it is one thing to accept the faithfulness of God as Divine truth, it is quite another to act upon it.[6]

In times of stress like preparing to depart, we found the need to lean on God. Carol and I would agree that, if you mapped out the ten most stressful times in our marriage, more than half of them would involve packing for our times to go back on the field. I don't know what it is about these times that set us off. But we eventually would come back to realizing that the stress was not worth it. As we stopped to consider the bigger picture, we could more clearly see God and trust him for what was coming.

One of the most important responses to God's faithfulness is hope. We hope because of who God is. Whenever I think of the word *hope*, I am

4. Tozer, *Knowledge of the Holy*, 78–79.
5. Tozer and Fessenden, *Attributes of God*, 2:164.
6. Pink, *Attributes of God*, 52.

instantly pulled to one of my favorite movies, *Shawshank Redemption* (based on the Stephen King short story *Rita Hayworth and the Shawshank Redemption*). Andy Dufrense is wrongfully sent to prison for the murder of his wife. He holds on to his hope, even though his new friend, Ellis "Red" Redding, tells him that "hope is a dangerous thing."[7] Andy responds, "Remember, Red, hope is a good thing, maybe the best of things, and no good thing ever dies." By the end of the movie, as Red is preparing to join Andy, he reflects, "I find I'm so excited, I can barely sit still or hold a thought in my head. I think it's the excitement only a free man can feel, a free man at the start of a long journey whose conclusion is uncertain. I hope I can make it across the border. I hope to see my friend and shake his hand. I hope the Pacific is as blue as it has been in my dreams. I hope."[8] One important difference in how Andy and Red use the word hope is helpful for us. Andy's hope was one of certainty, more than Red's hopefulness without certainty. When we trust in God, our hope is, indeed, certain.

DEPARTING WELL

A big part of that commissioning service for us was our opportunity to speak to the congregation. I had recently read a missionary biography of Jonathan Goforth. In it, he cited a missionary story of a family going to "darkest Africa." This was my first encounter with one of the "holding the rope" stories that are now told at commissioning services. In this version, the father took his wife and children to Africa. He challenged his church, saying that he would take his family into the dark hole of Africa if they, the church, would hold the rope in prayer. To make a long story short, his wife and children all died, and he was now deathly ill as well. Having made his way back to his sending church, he found his way to the back of the church during its prayer service. He sat quietly waiting to hear his name mentioned in prayer. That never happened. At the end of the service, he slowly walked up to the pulpit and rebuked the church. He said that the church had not held its end of the rope. They had not been faithful to uphold their responsibility to petition a faithful God on his family's behalf.[9]

Our church took this story to heart. We often received correspondence that ended with something along the lines of "tugging at this end." And one kind woman gave us some canned shortening. Between the plastic lid and the metal top, we found a coiled-up rope with a tag at one end that read,

7. Darabont, *Shawshank Redemption*, 1:08:25–1:09:38.

8. Darabont, *Shawshank Redemption*, 2:10:43–2:11:15.

9. Goforth, *Goforth of China*, 65–66.

"Holding the rope." To this day, more than thirty years later, that rope still hangs in my office as a reminder of our dependence on the prayers of others.

Good-byes are hard. And that's not a bad thing in itself. The apostle Paul experienced this pain as well. In Acts 20, we read the account of his saying good-bye to the church in Ephesus. I use this passage with my graduating seniors each semester. Carol and I also used it with our team leaders when we were preparing to say good-bye to them at the end of our missionary service. Paul concludes his farewell speech with a statement of entrusting them to God: "Now I commit you to God and to the word of His grace, which can build you up and give you an inheritance among all those who are sanctified" (Acts 20:32). I assure the graduating students that God will be faithful to them as they set out on their next chapter of serving him.

> Who is like you, LORD God Almighty? You, LORD, are mighty,
> and Your faithfulness surrounds You." (Ps 89:8)

God cannot not be faithful. It is his nature to be faithful at all times.

My favorite book of the Bible is Joshua. I have often taught through the book on the various short-term missions trip that Carol and I have led. It is rich in demonstrating God's attributes. As it relates to transitions in general and departures in particular, I am drawn to Joshua 24. Verse 15 is one of the most well-known: "But if serving the LORD seems undesirable to you, then choose for yourselves this day whom you will serve, whether the gods your ancestors served beyond the Euphates, or the gods of the Amorites, in whose land you are living. *But as for me and my household, we will serve the LORD.*"

But there would be no Joshua 24:15 if there weren't first Joshua 24:1–13, a rehearsal of God's faithfulness. Joshua details the many acts that demonstrate how God has watched over Israel. This, in turn, brings him to verse 14, a call to a response to God's faithfulness: "Now fear the LORD and serve Him with all faithfulness. Throw away the gods your ancestors worshiped beyond the Euphrates River and in Egypt, and serve the LORD." The response to God's faithfulness is a call to fear the Lord with our own faithfulness.

May I make a suggestion? How about writing your own Joshua 24:1–13, in which you detail all of the ways that God has shown himself to be faithful in your life? By doing this, it will become easier to trust him for the future, even when we sometimes fail to do so.

> Here is a trustworthy saying: If we died with Him, we will also live
> with Him; if we endure, we will also reign with Him. If we disown

Him, He will also disown us; if we are faithless, He remains faithful, for He cannot disown Himself." (2 Tim 2:11–13)

Your love, LORD, reaches to the heavens, Your faithfulness to the skies. (Ps 36:5)

Are you ready to go? God is! And he will faithfully look after you and those you love. Of what are you afraid? He is aware and able! He is aware of your challenges, and he is able to meet them head-on in a way that brings him glory and you hope.

QUESTIONS

1. What fears can you identify as you prepare to go (or when you recall preparing to go)? How does/did God's faithfulness speak to those fears?

2. What can your sending church and sending agency do to help send you well? What can *you* do to be better prepared to launch well?

3. What would your version of Joshua 24:1–13 look like? What would you list as examples of God's faithfulness over the past chapters of your life?

4. How can you model hope to those around you?

Chapter 5

Entry

God Is Always the Same, Even in Our Uncertainty

"Jesus Christ is the same yesterday and today and forever." (Heb 13:8)

"Now what does all this mean to you and me? It means that my poor, helpless, dependent self finds a home in God. God is our home!"

—A. W. TOZER[1]

I WANTED BANANAS. IT was just a few days into our time in Shanghai, and I decided to venture to the sidewalk market just outside of the campus where my wife and I taught English. I had seen who would become known for me as the Banana Lady. As I approached her, I knew full well that I was very vulnerable. I pointed to the bananas. She put some on the old-fashioned scales, the kind that has a long stick with a metal pan hanging on one end and a weight on the other. She said something to me which I supposed was the cost of the bananas. I dug into my pocket and pulled out some yuan and held out my hand. I had no idea how much she was charging or how much she was taking. I felt so stupid and helpless. And in my mind, I was saying something like, "You know, back in America, I was somebody."

---

1. Tozer and Fessenden, *Attributes of God*, 2:101.

And so it begins. Even though culture shock most likely will not hit until months into your arrival, the challenges of entering a new culture begin immediately. In fact, they begin before you even arrive. Unknown to you, you have carried some extra baggage with you when you arrived. Stereotypes go both ways. Before you can become known by others at a personal level, you are "known" by them in a generic manner. For example, if you are coming from the West, you are rich. So when you go to bargain at the market, trying to save the equivalent of twenty cents, you may be seen as insensitive to their need to make a living.

On top of that, you have to deal with your own set of expectations. Often, we do not even realize that we have an expectation until it isn't met. One such expectation became very clear to Carol and me early on. You need to know that my wife is an exceptional cook, and she is extremely resourceful when it comes to making due with what is available. This resourcefulness was born out of necessity when we arrived in Shanghai in January 1987. Our second week there, we were told that on Friday, we would be taken to the best Western supermarket where we could buy familiar foods. We were so excited to see what treasures would be found there. As you can imagine, we were sorely disappointed. When we got there, we were taken to the second floor of an old cement building to a room about the size and mood of an unfinished basement. The room was lined around three walls with metal shelves of canned goods. In short, it was a major disappointment. We left with a few cans of tomato paste but little else. We held it together until we got home but then had ourselves a good cry. It was just one of many episodes, some small and some bigger, of frustration or disappointment. Again, expectations and their impact on cultural adjustment.

DEALING WITH DISORIENTATION

Do you remember the camp game where you would put your forehead on an upright baseball bat and then be told to spin around several times before attempting to run to the next player in the relay race? The feeling of disorientation experienced when you first lift up your head from the bat is similar to what culture shock feels like. You feel like you should have this figured out. The goal of understanding this new culture is right there. But when you attempt to walk—forget about running—in the direction you want to go, you end up on the ground. You pick yourself up and try again. Eventually, after many sideways falls, you begin to regain your inner-ear orientation and more easily find your way forward.

And so it is with arriving in a new culture. This feeling of disorientation is normal. In fact, it might not even be a bad thing. It helps to accentuate that things are not the same as in your home culture. Things are changing all around you. From the simple things, like buying bananas, to the more complex things, like managing your visa, it takes so much energy just to get through a day.

Some like change more than others do. For those who like change, adjusting to a new culture can be an exciting adventure—at least, for a while. But for even the most daring ("Sure, I love trying new foods!"), a time comes when the loss of control and things familiar begins to cause stress levels to rise.

Now stress is not necessarily a bad thing, as most of us function better under some level of stress. And stressors can come in both positive and negative forms. Stress is our response to circumstances. We deal with stress by leaning on the One who never changes. "I the Lord do not change" (Mal 3:6).

Tozer recognized the value of this when he wrote, "What peace it brings to the Christian's heart to realize that our Heavenly Father never differs from Himself."[2] He asserts that God never gets better. That would imply change and that he could also get worse. This applies to *each* of his attributes!

> Chance and change are busy in our little world of nature and men, but in Thee we find no variableness nor shadow of turning. We rest in Thee without fear or doubt and face our tomorrows without anxiety. Amen.[3]

Culture Shock and Culture Stress

Culture adaptation tends to go through four stages. In the first stage, everything is exciting and fascinating. It's so much fun to explore the newness all around us. The second stage is where the shock comes in. It can hit anywhere between two and nine months. This is when we go from admiration to frustration. We may start to question why they do things the way they do, since our way of doing it is so much better (or so we think). Eventually, through God's help, we move on to a time of acceptance and, perhaps, appreciation for the cultural differences. Finally, we hopefully get to a place where we feel that this new way of living could actually be another home to us.

2. Tozer, *Knowledge of the Holy*, 53.
3. Tozer, *Knowledge of the Holy*, 49.

Culture shock sometimes hits us hard, even when we return for a second or subsequent term on the field. But culture shock comes and goes. Culture stress, on the other hand, is what we live with all of the time. I sometimes liken it to the lead vest worn at the dentist's office when having X-rays taken. After a while, you forget the weight on you—until you take it off. Culture stress is worn all the time. It only comes off when you leave your cross-cultural setting.

Some of the factors that contribute to culture stress could include the following: climate, having to bargain, communicating in a second language, the feeling of being watched (even bugged with listening devices!) all the time, living in a crowded (or secluded) place, lack of familiar foods, transportation (either driving yourself or having to get around on public transportation), confrontation styles, domestic help (or lack thereof), visa issues. The list goes on and on!

But in the midst of change, God remains the same.

> In God no change is possible; in men change is impossible to escape.[4]

> God allows things to change in order that He might establish that which cannot change.[5]

It was not unusual for me to hear someone state that they were having a "bad (insert local country) day." It became a simple way to express that their level of felt culture stress was higher at that moment than on other days. It was not necessarily a statement against the culture but more a request for some empathy.

At times of culture shock and culture stress, it becomes important to remember who God is. In particular, leaning on his immutability becomes a comfort. "What peace it brings to the Christian's heart to realize that our Heavenly Father never differs from Himself."[6] We find in God what we most need during times of change—a rock that remains solid and constant.

HE IS OUR HOME

"Now what does all this mean to you and me? It means that my poor, helpless, dependent self finds a home in God. God is our home!"[7]

4. Tozer, *Knowledge of the Holy*, 50.

5. Tozer and Fessenden, *Attributes of God*, 2:101.

6. Tozer, *Knowledge of the Holy*, 53.

7. Tozer and Fessenden, *Attributes of God*, 2:101.

There will come a time when the weight of having moved to a new culture will be felt ever so acutely. How will you respond? Will you trust in the never-changing God? Or will you allow thoughts of insecurity to rule?

For us, one of the stressors that was difficult for us was how our (then only) daughter was treated when we first arrived. The Chinese love children, especially foreign children. When we first arrived, she was thirteen months old. In order to become familiar with the campus (and to become familiar to those on campus), we took evening walks. It wasn't long before we learned a phrase that was constantly being used to describe her. It translates into "foreign doll." How cute, right? The problem was that she was treated as just that—a doll. They would touch her face, hair, and clothing. And they wanted to take her from us to show her off to their friends and family. We wrestled with how to respond. Should we allow this to happen in an effort to connect with the community? Should we err on the side of "protecting" our daughter? I'm sure we erred in extreme at both ends at times. It wasn't until Kara started to learn some Chinese and could express her own displeasure at being poked and squeezed that she was actually treated as a person and not simply as a doll.

How often is communication at the heart of handling stress in a cross-cultural experience? Probably most of the time, if we're honest. And what does it take for this new place to become home? One large factor is our ability to communicate with those around us. This is why, among other reasons, language learning *is* ministry.

Sometimes, in the midst of frustration, workers have asked for a quick trip home. When helping cross-cultural workers decide when to take their first trip back to their passport country, their home, one of the significant factors is how they are handling culture shock and culture stress. If they are not handling it well, I encourage them to *not* go home yet. The concern is that, if they leave the host culture with negative emotions, that is how they will think of this place whenever they think of returning. But if they are able to sustain themselves through culture shock and get to the place of seeing how this can now be called home, they are then at a healthy place to return to the passport country. That way, whenever they think about going back to their new home, they have more of a positive outlook about that return.

Creating Your New Home

One question that pops up regarding entry is whether or not the new missionaries should wade in the shallow water or jump into the deep water, so to speak. By this, it is meant that it might be advantageous to arrive in a place where culture and language learning can take place before going to the intended ministry location. The idea is that mistakes can be made without jeopardizing future ministry.

There should be a healthy balance sought between entering the culture in a way that helps cross-cultural workers engage with those they hope to minister versus shielding the new arrivers from the cultural challenges awaiting them.

Another reason for considering this strategy is to help with getting through culture shock and the related transitions. And one more issue, especially related to the current generation of new cross-cultural workers is the fear of a better offer (FOBO). Similar to FOMO (fear of missing out), FOBO manifests itself when commitments are broken because something better comes along. In the past few years, it seems to be increasingly seen that field workers, after a relatively short period of time, are opting to leave their teams to go to another ministry. This is not always bad, but it is almost always disruptive.

What sometimes comes into play here is not simply being redirected by God but an avoidance of the hard transition necessary to bond with the new culture. When the Banana Lady makes me feel like I'm a nobody, it isn't her doing at all. It's my allowing this to happen in my own mind. My felt loss of identity causes me to lose focus of my identity in Christ. I seek to find value in ways other than being a child of God.

When I'm having a "bad China day," it's not just that I'm experiencing the culture in a negative way. I'm leaning on my own perspective and not God's. And I'm seeing all the change around me and not the never-changing God and his ability to guide me through change.

Unconvinced that change is an ever-present reality? Just look at your social media page from a year ago. Now imagine doing the same for all of the people around you from the past year. Finally, if God had a social media page, remember that he *never* changes. It's because of this precious truth that we can embrace change and all that he wants to do in and through us in these times of disorientation.

Who we are before others will change. Who we are before God, Our Heavenly Father, never does. Because he is the same yesterday, today and forever, we can rest assured of who we are—even in times of change.

QUESTIONS

1. What do you think culture shock will look like for you? Have you experienced culture shock or culture stress before (e.g., going to college, moving to a new home, gaining or losing a family member)?

2. Where do you find your sense of identity, especially when under stress?

3. How do you need to rest on his immutability today? What is shifting sand in your life that drives you to an unchanging God? *What transitions are in front of you?*

4. How do you typically act when under stress?

Chapter 6

Adjusting to Team

God Is Gracious and Provides
Grace for Every Challenge

"The Word became flesh and made His dwelling among us. We have seen His glory, the glory of the One and only Son, who came from the Father, full of grace and truth." (John 1:14)

"Nowhere does the glory of God's free and sovereign grace shine more conspicuously than in the unworthiness and unlikeness of its objects."

—ARTHUR PINK[1]

ADJUSTING TO TEAM: BILL STRUGGLES WITH CULTURE

Carol and I were getting ready to board a flight out of Phnom Penh, Cambodia, where we had just concluded another visit to our team there. A couple of years earlier, on another such visit, my teammate Jeff accompanied me. We had heard that there was some conflict brewing on the team. Bill (not his

---

1. Pink, *Attributes of God*, 68.

real name) and his wife were the first non-Americans to join this established team, and we were told that some cross-cultural issues were causing conflict on the team.

It is not uncommon for new arrivals to struggle with the culture. This is expected. What is often not anticipated is the challenge of getting along with team members. Grace is needed for this relational adjustment, both by the new arrivals towards their team and for the new arrivals by their team members.

When we got there, we touched base with the team leader before going to Bill's home to listen to what his wife and he had to say. When we got to Bill's home, I purposed to extend grace by listening to all he had to say. In fact, for seven hours, we listened! I was determined to not speak until invited to do so. I wanted to make sure I heard all that they wanted to say. When finally given the opportunity to share some thoughts, I began by reflecting some of what we heard. But I also made the observation that most of the perceived differences were less about cultural differences and more about personality differences. Either way, discussions needed to be facilitated to help the team move forward in a positive manner.

A year later, the team was thriving. Bill and his wife, initially perceived to not be good team players, had become models of supportive and active team members. I would hold them up as jewels in how they blossomed on the team. All of the team members learned a lot through the process, and God continues to bless this team's efforts of church planting.

Dying to Self by Listening, Leaning on God's Grace

It was two years later when the airport scene happened. We had just completed yet another annual visit to the team. Without our knowing it, Bill's pastor from his home country had also been visiting them around the same time. But it wasn't until we met at the airport and were climbing up the stairs that he said to us, "I've heard about you. Bill says you're a good listener." Thank you, Lord! What a tremendous affirmation of following you by keeping my mouth shut. Dying to self by listening for as long as it takes is an act of grace made possible only by leaning on God's grace.

In the midst of cultural adaptation, even as you experience culture shock and culture stress, new relationships are being established. These include relationships with your team. And as you seek some measure of control in a fluid situation, sometimes your teammates take the brunt of your pride and selfishness. You have worked so hard to get to the field, which has taken a lot of effort and initiative. Now that you're with your new team, it is time to put some of that on the back burner as you get to know your new relationships and role.

When Does It Get to Be about Me?

Coming into a new situation, it can be easy for us to become self-centered. This was a trap that Bill had fallen into. We have so many needs, as I had heard from Bill and his wife, that we forget that in order to have good team-mates each of us needs to be a good teammate. This requires the ability to get out of yourself and to think about others and their needs. This is where God's grace comes in to play in our lives.

GOD'S GRACE—TO US AND THROUGH US

God's grace is all about his giving to us what we do not deserve. God helped me to extend grace to Bill and his wife through my listening. In turn, they learned to extend grace to their team. As such, it is a reflection of him and not of us. It points to the need for us to be humble, recognizing that we receive blessing upon blessing without earning anything. Of course, this begins and ends with our salvation and our relationship with the Living God. But he blesses us "with every spiritual blessing" (Eph 1:3) and with so much more!

When we fail to receive and live out God's grace, we tend toward pride and selfishness. It is imperative that new arrivals bring a learner's posture with them. My students graduate with a degree in intercultural studies. But it would be detrimental for their teams if they were to come in thinking that they know a better way of doing things simply because of their training.

How Good Are You at Receiving Grace?

According to Pink, "Nowhere does the glory of God's free and sovereign grace shine more conspicuously than in the unworthiness and unlikeness of its objects."[2] He goes on to state that this is foolishness to the world. Perhaps that is also why it is so powerful. When people receive grace, they usually know that they don't deserve it. It tends to have a ripple effect.

The first opportunity to show grace to others will most likely be with those you join in serving the Lord: your team. You may or may not have taken a survey trip. If you have, there is some familiarity with the members

2. Pink, *Attributes of God*, 68.

of the team. Perhaps some expectations have already been expressed. Maybe not. Regardless, you will arrive and soon find yourself wanting others to show grace to you. It is not unlike parents' asking for grace because their child is teething, sleepy, or tired from a long day.

How are you doing with receiving God's grace? I'll be honest with you. This is an area in which I struggled when I first came to Christ. Having been raised in a church-going family, I knew a lot about Jesus Christ. But I did not have a personal relationship with him. If you had asked me if I were I Christian, I would have replied in the affirmative. But then I was challenged with Ephesians 2:8–9:

> For it is by grace you have been saved, through faith—and this is
> not from yourselves, it is the gift of God—not by works, so that
> no one can boast.

You see, I had been taught that, if my good works outweighed my bad works, than I might have a hope to get into heaven. But as Paul makes clear, my good works were never going to be sufficient. That meant that I had to rely on God's grace through Jesus' death and resurrection if I wanted to truly have hope in being saved from the penalty of my sins. Next chapter we'll talk about mercy. But here, let's focus on his grace, giving what he wants to give because of who *he* is, not because of anything *I* am or have done.

Receiving Grace Is the Pathway to Giving Grace

This was something I had to grow in, both in my understanding and in my experience. Until we learn to receive God's grace, we cannot be expected to model grace to others. We often give to others, but usually with some sort of ulterior motive. As somebody whose primary love language is words of affirmation, I have struggled with giving to others in order to get those words. Giving grace means that it is done regardless of what is given in return. As Tozer said, "Grace is the good pleasure of God that inclines Him to bestow benefits upon the undeserving."[3] It flows from Jesus Christ to men. And "In olden times men looked forward to Christ's redeeming work; in later times they gaze back upon it, but always they came and they come by grace, through faith."[4]

It was only in learning to receive grace that I am able to extend grace. Sometimes that looks like dying to self through listening to others like Bill. Or it may come in the form of simply not needing to get your own way. At

3. Tozer, *Knowledge of the Holy*, 93.
4. Tozer, *Knowledge of the Holy*, 95.

the heart of being gracious is the ability to die to self, sometimes many times in a day.

Before moving on to talk about what this looks like when you first arrive, here are a few more verses about God's grace: John 1:16–17; Rom 3:22–24; 5:15, 20; Eph 1:6–8; 1 Pet 5:10.

Clearly, we are the blessed recipients of what we do not deserve, God's grace through Jesus Christ. But we also need to see how receiving God's grace is necessary to living the life God calls us to live for his glory. Especially in times of suffering, we lean on his grace. A lost and dying world needs to observe the hope we have through Christ so that they can be attracted to the Giver of Grace.

DYING TO SELF—A PATHWAY FOR MODELING GRACE TO OTHERS

One of the questions we need to ask ourselves is this: How many times a day am I willing to die to myself? Only when we are willing to die to our wants and desires can we begin to model God's grace to others.

Adjusting to Team: "This is not like my old team."

Jan had experienced burnout and had gone through an extensive time of healing and preparation for her next field of service. The Lord directed her to our team. It was a great fit. The more we spent time in preparing to receive her on the field, the more she remarked about how different things were from her previous experience. When asked about it, she explained how she felt much grace from our team. Initially, I was glad to hear her share this. But, as she continued to make this statement, the more I realized that she needed to move on in her/our new reality. I encouraged her to appreciate the grace she was enjoying but to attempt to refrain from repeated references to her previous experience. I felt that this kept her from moving on. She understood and made the adjustment.

We must start our grace journey by first recognizing our need for grace and how often we fail to experience grace. And then as we see God's grace at work in our lives, both in the past and present, we can transition from knowing and receiving his grace to sharing it with those around us. A trap we sometimes fall into is looking at the faults in others and convincing ourselves of why they don't deserve to be treated graciously. It is at precisely those moments that we need to hold up the mirror and remember how we are undeserving of God's grace. Only then will again receive his grace and be empowered by him to extend grace to others with humility.

Receiving Grace in Language Learning

One specific area where we need to receive grace from others and to extend grace to others is in the area of language learning. In my experience, there are two types of language learners: the gifted and the pluggers. I was a plugger and had to guard myself against envy of the gifted. I have also observed that some couples have one plugger and one gifted language learner. This can be a challenge for both, especially when serving in a shame-based culture. I remember feeling sorry for Carol when our Chinese teacher complimented me on my writing. To be fair, my handwriting—in any language—has been horrible. I have been called a doctor just because of my illegible writing. So when I wrote our Chinese characters in a similar way, while Carol wrote them nearly typewriter perfect, mine was seen as more like a local's. Okay, so I felt bad for Carol, but I also fought back some pride. But seriously, this is just a fun glimpse into what can be a significant struggle for some.

Extending Grace in Matters of Money

Another area where we need to be grace-filled with our teammates is in how money is spent. This is especially true with multicultural teams. For example, even something as simple as a team social event. For those who have an expectation of a nice night out, they may want to go to an expensive restaurant. Others may not have the financial means to do so but don't want to be seen as cheap or poor. It is important for expectations to be expressed and held loosely in times like these. For the new arrivers, it may take some time to realize that adjustments of their expectations will need to be made.

Remember Bill? To his credit, he exhibited great grace by embracing some hard conversations regarding his posturing on his new team. He and his team leader worked together to figure out a way for all on the team to feel heard and valued. This resulted in an even stronger team, one that went on to see a church-planting movement initiated in Cambodia. Additionally, Bill took the initiative to purchase an entire case of copies of a book that discussed working on a team with those from different cultures. He passed this book on to everyone on the team and beyond. The result was an increased level of understanding the issues, both related to culture and personality, involved in working in close proximity with others. Living out God's grace with each other continues to bring glory to God.

QUESTIONS

1. In addition to your salvation, how have you experienced God's grace in your own life?

2. What keeps you from extending grace to others?

3. In what areas of adjusting to cross-cultural ministry might you expect to need God's grace?

4. How have you expected grace from others?

Chapter 7

Adjusting to the Host Culture

God is Merciful to Us and through Us

"The LORD is compassionate and gracious, slow to anger, abounding in love." (Ps 103:8)

"Mercy is God's goodness confronting human guilt and suffering."

—A. W. TOZER[1]

SHE CAME BRINGING GIFTS. Within a couple of days of our arrival in Shanghai, Ms. Hu began to come to our on-campus apartment. Each time she came, she had another gift for us. At first, it was polite, and we appreciated her attempts to welcome us, albeit with her nearly nonexistent English. Mrs. Wang, our English department colleague, was the one tasked with helping us to get settled. With regards to Ms. Hu, we leaned heavily on Mrs. Wang to understand what was going on.

Mrs. Wang explained that gift-giving was a big part of the culture. We learned all about the Chinese word *guanxi*, the principle of reciprocity. It was important to not let the "*guanxi* account" build up. The more you received from somebody, the more you were indebted to that person. Giving a gift of similar value to the one you received needed to be done sooner than later.

---

1. Tozer and Fessenden, *Attributes of God*, 2:85.

The problem was that we had not caught on to this until it was too late with regard to Ms. Hu. Again, we were new to the culture, and we didn't yet speak Mandarin. By the time we understood what was happening, Ms. Hu was already pleading with us to help her to get a visa to the USA. Carol and I had already decided that we would not be a part of sponsoring or helping anyone, knowing that this would open up an expectation that would result in a possible flood of requests. When we refused to help Ms. Wu to get to the USA, she stepped up her efforts through bigger gifts. The more we refused her gifts, the angrier she got. It got so bad that I once had to physically push her out of our apartment. This was not culturally appropriate, but Mrs. Wang consoled us by telling us that Ms. Hu had gone beyond what was culturally acceptable in her persistence with us. We understood that Ms. Hu was acting out of desperation, but we felt very much abused by her.

This feeling of abuse was to be repeated during our many years in Southeast Asia. It is a fine line to walk when you want to believe the best of others, yet need to protect yourself from those who simply want to use "the foreigner." How do you model Christ in times like these? At a time when you want to build strong relationships with those you came to serve, you also open yourself up to being hurt.

HOW DO I SEE THEM?

When you enter a new culture or location, you tend to see people in one of three ways. First, you may see them as scenery. Imagine that you've just arrived at the airport in New Delhi, India. After you manage your way through immigration and customs, you fight your way to a taxi and head towards your guest house. As you drive through the city, you take in the sights. There's a Hindu temple. Oh, look! There's a McDonalds! I wonder if they serve beef. (They don't.) Along the way, you see some beggars at the intersection. When you see them in a similar light as the temple and McDonalds, you are seeing them as scenery.

Second, you will see some people as utility. The driver of your taxi may fall into this category. You see him as someone who will help you to, in this case, get from the airport to your guest house. Whether it be due to your lack of Hindi or being tired or some other reason, you simply use this taxi driver for your purpose. Now don't get me wrong. This is not necessarily a bad thing. We only have so much emotional energy at a given time. We rarely have what would be needed to engage each person all the time of every day. We make choices.

But how often do we allow ourselves to see others as people, the third way to see people, and not just as scenery or utility? And, at the same time, we need to realize that the locals are making the same choice with regards to us! Some may see us as scenery, wanting to touch the "foreign doll's" face or hair. Some, like Ms. Hu, will see us as utility. And some, thank the Lord, will see us as people.

The challenge is that we are usually unaware of these choices, both by us and about us, when we first arrive. We are perhaps in that state of disorientation where all we are trying to do is get our own bearings. As mentioned in the last chapter, we tend to be more selfish at times like these.

When you feel like you are having a bad (country) day, ask yourself if you have allowed yourself to see those around you as scenery or utility. Perhaps taking a moment to see them as people will help to gain some perspective. This is where mercy may need to be exercised. One of my former pastors used to say that we need to not expect lost people to act as those who are walking closely with the Lord. Lost people should be expected to act as lost people. Our response to being used or abused needs to have at least a measure of tolerance, patience, and mercy. Otherwise, we will find anger rising within us.

Handling Anger

I confess to having anger issues. This is an area in which God has had to work on me ever since I came to Christ. I have failed miserably many times, as my family can attest. I have seen the harm that anger causes in relationships. Perhaps because of this, I have also become very sensitive to anger. I have studied it in myself and others. I have found that anger often is a response to a blocked goal or a response to shame or perceived shame. It is interesting that my anger is more often a response to the latter than the former.

When I reflect on when I would get angry overseas, I can see how it was usually because I felt like I was being taken advantage of or being shamed in some way. Even thinking back to Banana Lady and how I felt so helpless buying bananas, I recognize the level of shame I felt and how anger would rise up within me.

I remember going to get a visa to visit our workers in India. I went to an Indian consulate in Thailand and filled out all the necessary paperwork. When I was called to the window to pay for the visa, I was given an amount nearly double what a non-American was required to pay. I asked for an explanation. I was told that they were simply treating Americans the way the

American government treated Indians. And they were right! I paid the visa fee, along with the American surcharge, and went on my way. I thank the Lord for his helping me to control my anger, as getting angry would have resulted in no visa and a blot on my testimony of the Lord.

It is not a question of whether or not we will experience injustice or unfairness. We will. But what do we do with our anger when it happens? I will discuss injustice more in a later chapter. For now, the main concern is how to handle the anger inside of us, especially when it is directed at those we came to serve.

MERCY IS A CHOICE

I sure am glad God doesn't treat me the way I deserve to be treated by him. Last chapter, the focus was on God's grace. As God blesses us, it is so that we can bless others. Mercy is sometimes seen as being on the opposite side of grace on God's coin of how he treats us. Whereas God demonstrates his grace by giving us what we do not deserve, he demonstrates his mercy by not giving us what we do deserve. "While were still sinners, Christ died for us" (Rom 5:8). As a sinner, I deserve death, not life.

> Praise be to the God and Father of our Lord Jesus Christ! In his great mercy he has given us new birth into a living hope through the resurrection of Jesus Christ from the dead. (1 Pet 1:3)

God has every right to punish us for our sins. Yet he is merciful. Why? At least in part, it is so that we will, in turn, be merciful to others. But it starts with our knowing his mercy. "To receive mercy we must first know that God is merciful."[2] Take a moment to read through Ps 103:8–14.

Being merciful does not mean you are unaware of or ignore an offense. On the contrary, it is being completely aware and yet choosing to not act on the offense. "Mercy cannot cancel judgment apart from atonement. When justice sees iniquity, there must be judgment. But mercy brought Christ to the cross . . . All men are recipients of the mercy of God, but God has postponed the execution, that is all."[3] Even in the giving of the Ten Commandments, God demonstrates his mercy:

> So Moses chiseled out two stone tablets like the first ones and went up Mount Sinai early in the morning, as the Lord had commanded him; and he carried the two stone tablets in his hands. Then the Lord came down in the cloud and stood there with him

2. Tozer, *Knowledge of the Holy*, 92.
3. Tozer, *Knowledge of the Holy*, 86.

and proclaimed his name, the Lord. And he passed in front of Moses, proclaiming, "The Lord, the Lord, the compassionate and gracious God, slow to anger, abounding in love and faithfulness, maintaining love to thousands, and forgiving wickedness, rebellion and sin. Yet he does not leave the guilty unpunished; he punishes the children and their children for the sin of the parents to the third and fourth generation." (Exod 34:4–7)

We will examine God's justice in chapter 9, but our focus here is God's mercy and how we need to help others see how mercy is lived out in our lives. This can be done as we forgive others. "You, Lord, are forgiving and good, abounding in love to all who call to you" (Ps 86:5).

Are you able to catch yourself when your anger rises within you? "But I tell you, love your enemies and pray for those who persecute you, that you may be children of your Father in heaven. He causes his sun to rise on the evil and the good, and sends rain on the righteous and the unrighteous" (Matt 5:44–45).

WHY WE EXTEND MERCY—NOT BECAUSE OF THEM

We are not merciful because of those who offend us. We have to be careful that we don't mistakenly base our motive on our desire to see them come to Christ. Rather, we reflect Christ to bring glory to God. As they see Christ in us, they will be drawn to God. We want them to be drawn to God and not to us.

In the early days of ministry in a new culture, it is easy to get upset with those around us. One temptation to be avoided is to tell fun stories at the expense of the nationals. This sometimes happens at team meetings in an attempt to feel better about ourselves. This does not reflect well on us or on God. But it is so easy to do, especially when we feel that we have been mistreated or shamed in some way.

One of our American team leaders serving in South Asia was teaching English when the USA was attacked on 9/11. In this Muslim context, his class cheered at the news. How would you have responded at that moment? If the first thought were personal, anger would be the natural response. But if God's mercy can be considered, there is the possibility that a merciful response can be generated. This is impossible apart from the work of the Holy Spirit and the knowledge of God's desire that all come to know him.

The Lord is not slow in keeping his promise, as some understand slowness. Instead he is patient with you, not wanting anyone to perish, but everyone to come to repentance. (2 Pet 3:9)

One of the best stories I ever heard that demonstrates this is the beloved Pineapple Story. I first heard the story from Otto Koning's son when his family visited us in Hong Kong.

Otto Koning and his wife, Carol, went to Irian Jaya (New Guinea) to be missionaries. They worked among a native tribe that had only known their village ways. One of those village ways was stealing from others. When Otto and his wife arrived and moved into a hut, the natives often came by to visit. The Konings would notice that after they left that various household items had disappeared. They saw these items again when they went to preach in the natives' village.

The only fruit Otto could grow on the island was pineapples. Otto loved pineapples and took pride in the ones he grew. However, whenever they began to ripen, the natives stole them. Otto could never keep a ripe pineapple for himself. This was frustrating and he became angry with the natives. All during the seven-year period in which this took place, Otto preached the gospel to these natives but never had a conversion.

The more the natives stole, the angrier Otto became.

Otto took a furlough to the United States and attended a conference on personal rights. At this conference, he discovered that he was frustrated over this situation because he had taken personal ownership of his pineapple garden. After much soul-searching, he gave his garden to God. Soon the natives started having problems among their tribe. The natives saw a correlation between what Otto had done and their own lives being affected by calamities in their village.

When Otto gave his garden to God, he no longer got angry and was free from worry. The natives started bringing him fruit from the garden because they didn't want any more calamities to come into their village.

The light came on one day when a native said to Otto, "Tuan (sir), you have become a Christian. You don't get angry anymore. We always wondered if we would ever meet a Christian."

They had never associated Otto with the kind of person he was preaching about because his message did not line up with his life. Otto was broken in spirit when he realized he had been such a failure.

At the end of seven years, he witnessed his first conversion, and many began coming to Christ once he fully gave his garden to God. The fruit grew so abundantly and his village became the most evangelized in the whole region.[4]

It is important when we are wronged to maintain an eternal mindset. How can these times become opportunities to show the mercy of God? What will it take within us to respond in a God-honoring way? You will have your own stories of how you will feel wronged, abused, and shamed. How you respond at those times will impact your ministry for a long time to come. Will you become angry and vengeful?

The Chinese have a proverb that translates roughly as "A good beginning is halfway there." May God help you to make a good beginning as you seek to reflect his mercy to those around you.

QUESTIONS

1. In the last month, how have you (or could you have) benefited from mercy from others?

2. In the last month, what opportunities have you had to demonstrate God's mercy to others?

3. In what types of situations or circumstances might you be susceptible to anger?

4. Do you tend to be tolerant of others' behavior? How might you do even better in this area?

4. Koning, "Pineapple Story," paras. 2–8.

PART 3

On-field Ministry

Chapter 8

Connecting with the People

*God Is Already There and Knows
the Best Way Forward*

"I have become all things to all people so that by all means I might save some."
(1 Cor 9:22b)

"Wisdom, among other things, is the ability to devise perfect ends and to
achieve those ends by the most perfect means. It sees the end from the beginning, so there can be no need to guess or conjecture."

—A. W. Tozer[1]

"But what should I do?"

It's not unusual for those who have finally arrived on the field to realize
that they are unprepared to connect with those that live around them in
a meaningful way. When Carol and I first arrived, we took evening walks
around the campus. This helped our neighbors to get to know us and us
to get to know them. Even with our nonexistent language skills, we could
communicate with those who had patience with us.

We quickly discerned that early evening was family time in the community. We found this to be true in all three Asian countries where we lived.

---

1. Tozer, *Knowledge of the Holy*, 60.

The best time to connect with them was immediately after dinner. Unfortunately, I have seen many cross-cultural workers living overseas, especially those from the West, claim post-dinner time as *their* family time. In my opinion, it would benefit them to come to an understanding that opportunities like these are precious and ought to be utilized.

Likewise, I have often heard my students refer to FOMO, or Fear Of Missing Out. This is sometimes demonstrated by their making changes to their schedules in what feels to me like a rash manner. I would actually change it to FOBO, or the Fear Of a Better Offer. For example, when we have a scheduled event, it is not unusual to have one or more students cancel at the last minute because something else that they felt was a better offer came up.

As mentioned earlier, on the mission field, something similar is increasingly happening. With greater frequency, cross-cultural field workers are arriving on the field and, within a relatively short period of time, deciding to change teams or ministries. This is part of the reason that more and more agencies are developing launch teams, those that have new workers go through orientation and language learning on these teams for the first one to two years. During this time, exploration into ministry opportunities is made before joining a specific team.

All of this calls us back to the question, "What should I do?" Wisdom is essential to discern which of the many (or few) opportunities present themselves to the worker. Innovation and flexibility, one of our agency's core values, should be coupled with a heavy dependence on God's wisdom.

This needs to be combined with a God-given understanding of what will bless those we hope to minister to. All too often, cross-cultural workers go in with an assumption of what will bless others without having sufficient perspective. In Duane Elmer's book, *Cross-cultural Servanthood*, he shares the story of the monkey and the fish. In short, the monkey feels good about how he "rescued" the fish from the floodwaters, citing how it became very calm (dead) after being placed on dry land. Likewise, cross-cultural workers are sometimes guilty of misguided attempts to bless others. Sometimes these well-intentioned acts of kindness have the opposite effect, even to the detriment of future ministry. Again, we should seek God's wisdom and discernment before making decisions about how to minister to others. God is already there and working. We need his mind to know how he wants us to join in what he is doing.

GOD'S WISDOM FOR MINISTRY CONNECTION: "FOR MY THOUGHTS ARE NOT YOUR THOUGHTS"

My students and others sometimes tell me that they appreciate my wisdom. I jokingly respond that they're just saying I am old. There is some truth in that, as much of what I share is informed by experiences that God has given me. But there is also an element of listening and discernment that is also God-given.

When it comes to seeking God's wisdom regarding ministry opportunities, we must recognize that gaining knowledge is only part of wisdom. Wisdom refers more to knowing what to do with knowledge. "It is vitally important that we hold the truth of God's infinite wisdom as a tenet of our creed; but this is not enough. We must by the exercise of our faith and by prayer bring it into the practical world of our day-to-day experience."[2]

God's wisdom is not added to our wisdom. Rather, we seek and depend upon God's wisdom in place of our own wisdom. For this to be our reality, we must recognize what godly wisdom is. As Tozer comments,

> Wisdom, among other things, is the ability to devise perfect ends and to achieve those ends by the most perfect means. It sees the end from the beginning, so there can be no need to guess or conjecture.[3]

And again,

> Wisdom in the Bible is different from wisdom on earth, in that Bible wisdom has a moral connotation. It is high and holy, full of love and purity.[4]

As with many of God's attributes, his wisdom connects with other attributes. In this case, his omniscience (knowing all things) informs his wisdom. And so it should be with us. The more we learn about God and our situation, the easier it is to lean on his wisdom to know what to do for his glory. When we ask what we are to do in a new culture and ministry, God will answer our request to give us wisdom. Sometimes, this is a matter of discerning his best over what we perceive to be good.

How many times do we settle for the good right in front of us when God has something better for us? This often happens mid-way through language learning. A ministry opportunity may present itself. It might be an opportunity that does not require full language skills. The cross-cultural worker may be feeling frustrated with not doing ministry yet, so he agrees to

2. Tozer, *Knowledge of the Holy*, 62–63.
3. Tozer, *Knowledge of the Holy*, 60.
4. Tozer and Fessenden, *Attributes of God*, 2:131.

this opportunity. At this moment, two things might happen. First, language learning slows down or even halts. Secondly, if and when the originally desired level of language is attained, it becomes difficult to disengage in the ministry already undertaken. This, in turn, makes it difficult to take up the original ministry for which language learning was started. The decision to agree to the earlier ministry opportunity may be short-sighted and lacking in wisdom and may be done to stroke one's ego and make the person feel like they are doing "real ministry." One way to combat this temptation is to recognize that, as I drill into my students, "language learning *is* ministry." Again, God's wisdom needs to be aggressively pursued in times like this.

God's wisdom is to be sought as a gift. It is a wisdom that has been demonstrated by what God has done. "By wisdom the LORD laid the earth's foundations, by understanding he set the heavens in place; by his knowledge the watery depths were divided, and the clouds let drop the dew" (Prov 3:19–20)

Scripture repeatedly reminds us of the deep chasm between God's wisdom and ours:

> 'For my thoughts are not your thoughts, neither are your ways my ways,' declares the LORD. 'As the heavens are higher than the earth, so are my ways higher than your ways and my thoughts than your thoughts.' (Isa 55:8–9)

> Oh, the depth of the riches of the wisdom and knowledge of God! How unsearchable his judgments, and his paths beyond tracing out! 'Who has known the mind of the Lord? Or who has been his counselor?' (Rom 11:33–34)

God Desires That We Seek His Wisdom

And it pleases the Lord to hear us ask for his wisdom. To Solomon, after asking God for wisdom instead of riches, God said, "I will give you a wise and discerning heart" (1 Kgs 3:12). Asking God for wisdom was an indication of Solomon's understanding of how precious it is. We need to come to terms with how our own wisdom is insufficient to handle life's big questions.

This presupposes that we are walking closely with God. Otherwise, hearing his wisdom will be difficult, if not impossible. God wants to give us his wisdom, but he also expects us to ask for it. Perhaps one of the more well-known passages used for this is the following:

Consider it pure joy, my brothers and sisters, whenever you face trials of many kinds, because you know that the testing of your faith produces perseverance. Let perseverance finish its work so that you may be mature and complete, not lacking anything. If any of you lacks wisdom, you should ask God, who gives generously to all without finding fault, and it will be given to you. But when you ask, you must believe and not doubt, because the one who doubts is like a wave of the sea, blown and tossed by the wind. That person should not expect to receive anything from the Lord. Such a person is double-minded and unstable in all they do. (Jas 1:2–8)

I include the whole passage for context. As I understand verse 5 in its context, God is saying that his wisdom is given to help us to understand what he is doing in the midst of our trials. In short, we get his perspective. That is not to say that he doesn't give us wisdom in the form of knowing what to do; he does. But in this passage, his wisdom helps us to understand our trials in a way that demonstrates why a higher view will comfort and guide us.

Having said that, Scripture makes it clear that God does desire that we seek his wisdom to know what to do, whether in response to what we are experiencing or with regard to what we could pursue (Prov 2:6; 3:5–7).

Wisdom and action go together. Knowledge alone is powerless. It is only when applied to action that it demonstrates wisdom. "But wisdom is proved right by her deeds" (Matt 11:19).

So how do we get God's wisdom? First, we must desire it. This begins with acknowledging our wisdom as being lacking and God's wisdom as being superior and perfect. Then we need to spend time in God's word and in prayer, allowing God to speak to us in his truth and Spirit. Listening prayer is a big part of this, as we have to stop talking and wait upon him to speak. And we should enter times like these with open eyes and an open mind, not presupposing what God will say.

WISDOM TO CONNECT—THAT I MIGHT WIN SOME

In addition to going on evening strolls around campus when we first arrived in China, we soon realized that connecting with our students was going to happen best outside of the classroom. We wanted to become part of the community and to get a feel for what God wanted us to do beyond simply teaching English.

The longer we were in China, the easier it was to see how some groups associated with some more than others. This is true everywhere, I suppose. But sometimes it takes some time to discern this. David Hesselgrave, in

Communicating Christ Cross-culturally, raises two questions for the newly arrived cross-cultural worker. The first is this: *Who am I to them?*[5] They are looking to put me in a box. This is why, when I first got in a taxi in Shanghai, I would be asked several questions about who I am. Some questions were predictable, like, "Where are you from?" Others were slightly uncomfortable, like, "How much money do you make?" And then there was the one that took me a little while to figure out: "How old are you?" It wasn't until I understood enough Mandarin and culture that I realized that different words are used to address one another based on age. By knowing my age, they knew whether to call me older brother or younger brother, for example. When learning my occupation (English teacher), they found it easier to respect me.

The second question Hesselgrave says we should address is: *Who are they to each other?*[6] This is very important, as deciding to associate with one group may jeopardize being able to connect with another group. Our friends who chose to work with those in the slums outside of Bangkok would not have also been able to work with the businessmen of downtown Bangkok. This is something that needs to be recognized and acted upon when you first arrive. To jump into ministry prematurely and without wisdom may have negative implications for future ministry opportunities.

Carol and I wanted to become part of the community, especially that of our students. We wanted to live out Paul's exhortation to "become all things to all people so that by all means I might save some" (1 Cor 9:22b).

Wisdom That Leads to Becoming Part of the Community

Since Carol and I felt called to minister to our students, we made decisions about how to connect with them. This included playing basketball and volleyball with them in the afternoons. But it also included having them to our home for Carol's great cooking and to watch a movie with us. This was something that set us apart from how students normally connected with their teachers. Years later, our students affirmed how these times with them helped them to hear us talk about life issues. Since we were in their lives, they trusted us with heart-level conversations.

We felt led by God to live our lives in close proximity to our students. This goes against prevailing wisdom to avoid dual relationships. As teachers, we are told to not create situations where, for example, students babysit your children. This would lead to potential favoritism. This is wise. However, I have found that such wisdom is not universal. There are times

---

5. Hesselgrave, *Communicating Christ Cross-culturally*, 460.

6. Hesselgrave, *Communicating Christ Cross-culturally*, 460.

when building community with students provides opportunities to impact students in ways that have nothing to do with teaching. Carol and I have lived this out in our years in China as well as here at Lancaster Bible College.

One example of doing this in China was our hiring of students to wash dishes after our evening meal. We found this to be a good way to give Carol more time outside of the kitchen, to give students additional income, and to impact students in a more personal manner. One such student was "Maxene" (her chosen English name for class). She washed our dishes for one academic year, and she got to know our family really well. Later on, she would share with us how the seven girls in her dorm room would often talk about our marriage. They admired how we loved each other. This, in turn, gave us an opportunity to talk about the love of Jesus. To make a long story shorter, Maxene came to Christ and brought all of her dormmates to our home to hear the gospel message. Maxene went from dishwasher to disciple-maker. Had we followed man's wisdom of avoiding dual relationships, rather than God's wisdom of connecting with our students, we may have missed a tremendous ministry opportunity.

We also recognize that having integrity to who we say we are is vitally important. We were English teachers. We consider this what is called a tent-making ministry. By that, it is meant that an occupation is used to both create a local identity as well as income to minimize the need for support from outside sources. As a matter of integrity, if you are going to make tents, make good tents. Pioneers wisely counseled me to get my Master's degree in Teaching English as a Second Language, which I did before we left for China. Carol and I worked hard to be the best English teachers we could be. We also were diligent to be seen as English teachers, including attending English Corners on campus, where anyone on campus could come to practice speaking English with a native English speaker. We were diligent to do our best to help our students, including helping to prepare them to get good jobs after graduation. Our efforts were rewarded in a tangible way when the city of Shanghai awarded us with the White Magnolia Award, having been nominated by our university officials. We felt that this strengthened our integrity as well as our identity among the community.

Of course, we have not always made wise decisions. There was that one time in 1989, just six months after the Tiananmen Square protests were brutally shut down, that we did what we had done the previous December. We introduced the students to Christmas caroling and walked them around the campus housing. It was only about ten minutes into this fun event that the dean of our department quickly came to us and told us we must shut it down immediately. He pointed out that what we were doing could easily be misinterpreted as a student demonstration. Oh my! Needless to say, we ushered the students into a classroom and continued our caroling privately.

And please understand that there are times when it is God-honoring to change plans. There have been a number of times when I have observed that God redirects people to places and ministries. However, these are more the exception than the norm. FOBO must not be the determining factor for leaving a previous commitment. The desire should be for God's leading as the best opportunity. As was discussed in chapter 1, this includes utilizing all the resources available (God's word, God's people, prayer, circumstances, etc.) when making significant decisions.

A good example of following the Lord's leading was a family who felt God's call to serve in a communist country in Southeast Asia. They arrived with an idea of how they were going to have a lasting identity there, dealing with art. That lasted a couple of years, but that time was when God helped them to see a much more sustainable presence, one that gave them many more ministry opportunities. As they followed the Lord's leading, step by step over a few years, they found themselves impacting many families through their own efforts and those of team members they were able to bring along. The point is that following the Lord's leading, with his wisdom, sometimes takes time and availability. It is not impulsive.

> With the goodness of God to desire our highest welfare, the wisdom of God to plan it, and the power of God to achieve it, what do we lack? Surely we are the most favored of all creatures.[7]

We rob ourselves and others when we rely solely on our own understanding. May God give us the desire to seek him and his wisdom. He is already at work at the places we are going. Let us ask him to see what he is doing and get in on it.

QUESTIONS

1. Can you remember a time when you felt you understood a situation only to realize you messed up? What would you have done differently?

2. List 3 to 5 areas in your life right now where you should ask God for wisdom.

3. Can you think of an example of man's wisdom that might not agree with God's wisdom?

4. What role does common sense play in discerning God's plans for your life?

---

7. Tozer, *Knowledge of the Holy*, 64.

Chapter 9

Serving Others

God Is Loving, Merciful, and Just; and Our Ministry Should Be as Well

"He has told you, O man, what is good. And what does the LORD require of you? To act justly and to love mercy and to walk humbly with your God." (Mic 6:8)

"Love wills the good of all and never wills harm or evil to any."

—A. W. TOZER[1]

"When we speak of God as transcendent we mean of course that He is exalted far above the created universe, so far above that human thought cannot imagine it. To think accurately about this, however, we must keep in mind that 'far above' does not here refer to physical distance from the earth but to quality of being. We are concerned not with location in space nor with mere altitude, but with life."

—A. W. TOZER[2]

---

1. Tozer, *Knowledge of the Holy*, 98.
2. Tozer, *Knowledge of the Holy*, 69.

Body or soul? When I first started my role as Area Leader, overseeing our teams in Southeast Asia, our team in Cambodia was just getting started. As the team was getting its feet wet, the team leader found himself in a discussion about how to prioritize ministry opportunities. Those who were already working there were somewhat polarized into two groups, each claiming to be doing God's work. On the one hand were those focused on community development. They felt that the priority needed to be on meeting the many physical needs of the people. On the other hand, the church planters were convinced that it was the spiritual needs that should be most important. Our team leader wisely recognized that this did not need to be an either/or proposition.

Instead, there should be some way to incorporate a both/and approach. The church-planting team found ways to address medical and educational needs of the poor as part of their ministry strategy. They spent time in their first term on the field observing what was happening and exploring possibilities. As language skills were developed, connections were made. After moving to a provincial capital and, later, a smaller village, the wife of the team leader embarked on a program to help poor families. The CHOW program was designed to help children, including orphans, and widows. This help came in the form of such things as rice and assistance for school (tuition and supplies). Soon after the first church in the movement was planted, the administration of the CHOW program was handed over to the church.

Concurrently, God led a doctor to join the team. As his language skills developed, he came alongside the local clinic and humbly made his services available. He avoided the temptation to come in as the answer to all their needs. This opened doors for him to make visits to homes in the remote village where the team was hoping to bring the gospel. His demonstration of God's love through his meeting medical needs helped those on the team prepared to tell stories about God's love through the life of Jesus. It was a blessing for me to watch this process unfold and to see a church-planting movement begun in this province.

Upon returning to the USA, I soon began to have the wonderful privilege of being involved in the Frontier Ventures course *Perspectives on the World Christian Movement*. *Perspectives* is a 15-week course offered around the world that gives a solid introduction to missions through four perspectives: biblical, historical, cultural, and strategic. This fourth perspective, strategic, begins with a lesson on Christian community development and is followed by two lessons on church planting. One of the articles that students read is Samuel Moffett's "Evangelism: The Leading Partner." The discussion is the same as the one in Cambodia, to seek first to meet physical or spiritual needs?

RESPONDING TO FELT NEEDS

In the previous chapter, the emphasis was on seeking God's wisdom so as to not simply follow our own understanding of how to prepare to minister in a new cross-cultural environment. In this chapter, I want to take it a step further by examining how God sees the needs of others. This will, Lord willing, help us to be better postured to respond to the needs of those we seek to see impacted by Christ.

We could ask which of God's attributes of love, justice, or transcendence is more important. The answer, of course, is that none is more important than the others. However, these three do come to bear on decisions that are made regarding ministry strategy. God's love motivates us to meet needs of all kinds. His justice demands that we respond to the injustices we see in the world. And his transcendence calls us to see how the Lord is above all in a way that encompasses a view of all needs and resources. This results in compassion and boldness as opposed to arrogance and timidity.

> What is most important in the life of the church is its mission. . . . Sometimes we limit the mission of the church to that which it does when it looks outward, calling sinners, serving the needy, preaching in distant lands. But the inner life of the church is also part of its mission. It is in the inner life that we learn to practice a love that goes beyond the social, economic, cultural, and political links that govern social relations. That inner life of the church immediately becomes an outward witness. As Jesus himself said, 'By this everyone will know that you are my disciples, if you love one another' (John 13:35). And somewhat later, in the midst of persecutions late in the second century and early in the third, Tertullian tells us that pagans said about Christians, 'See how they love one another.' The heart of the mission of the church is giving witness to the purpose of God for all of creation.[3]

When I was in college, Josh McDowell spoke on campus about love and dating. It prompted me to write an article in the school newspaper in which I suggested that true love is spelled G-I-V-E. Love seeks to give rather than to get. In today's world, at least in much of American culture, we seem to value kindness and respect more than love. But the motivation for this is often one of anger at being disrespected. This results in love being redefined as not being bad to others. But love is so much more.

---

3. González, *Knowing Our Faith*, 94–95.

God's Love in a Hurting World

Perhaps the most well-known Bible verse in the USA is John 3:16, thanks in part to its reference being lifted up in many sporting events for others to see. It begins with, "For God so loved the world that . . . ." The word *that* is highly significant. I actually wrote a paper on the history of the word *that* for my History of the English Language class for my Master's degree. It is a demonstrative pronoun. In other words, it more fully demonstrates the phrase before it. (One of my favorite sentences from that paper is "He said that that *that* that I used was wrong.) Anyway, in John 3:16, what comes after the *that* points to the phrase before it. In this case, we have a better understanding of God's love because it is demonstrated by the phrase "that He gave his one and only Son." Notice the verb that demonstrates love: *gave*. God's giving of his Son reveals how he loved us.

Furthermore, if you go to 1 John 4:7–21, you see an expanded passage of John 3:16. A quick look at the nouns and verbs reflects God's love for the world and how that love is acted out through the giving of his Son for our salvation. We see in this passage that "God is love" (v. 16), and that "We love because he first loved us (19), and this results in our loving others (21). The progression is clear. Until we live in God's love, we cannot and will not love others in a God-empowered manner.

> The words, 'God is love," mean that love is an essential attribute of God. Love is something true of God but it is not God . . . . Because God is self-existent, His love had no beginning; because He is eternal, His love can have no end; because He is infinite, it has no limit; because He is holy, it is the quintessence of all spotless purity; because He is immense, His love is an incomprehensibly vast, bottomless, shoreless sea before which we kneel in joyful silence and from which the loftiest eloquence retreats confused and abashed.[4]

Perhaps the vastness of God's love is why Paul prayed that we would more fully know it.

> For this reason I kneel before the Father, from whom every family in heaven and on earth derives its name. I pray that out of his glorious riches he may strengthen you with power through his Spirit in your inner being, so that Christ may dwell in your hearts through faith. And I pray that you, being rooted and established in love, may have power, together with all the Lord's holy people, to grasp how wide and long and high and deep is

---

4. Tozer, *Knowledge of the Holy*, 98.

the love of Christ, and to know this love that surpasses knowledge—that you may be filled to the measure of all the fullness of God. (Eph 3:14–19)

In our souls, we long for this kind of relationship. "One of our greatest needs as human beings is to be loved . . . . When we doubt that we are loved, we may develop unacceptable behavior patterns to compensate for it."[5] Again, our views of love can become skewed from true, godly love. This can result in pursuing harmful vices such as alcohol, drugs, self-harm, overeating, etc. "Whenever you are tempted to doubt the love of God, Christian reader, go back to Calvary."[6] It is at the Calvary cross that we see God's love. "But God demonstrates his own love for us in this: While we were still sinners, Christ died for us." (Rom 5:8)

When we look for ministry opportunities, God's love should motivate us to love others.

> We see it showing itself as good will. Love wills the good of all and never wills harm or evil to any.[7]

> It is of the nature of love that it cannot lie quiescent. It is active, creative, and benign . . . God does not love populations, He loves people.[8]

God's Justice in a Broken World

A second attribute of God that comes to bear on pursuing ministry opportunities is his justice. This is often combined with his holiness and wrath, recognizing that "He will by no means leave the guilty unpunished" (Exod 34:7). Justice issues have come to the forefront in the past two decades, including such atrocities as human trafficking, genocide, homelessness, child abuse, and hunger. When justice is present, the world is as it should be. "Will not the Judge of all the earth do right?" (Gen 18:25). God's being Judge does not necessitate his being subjectively angry.

> Justice, when used of God, is a name we give to the way God is, nothing more; and when God acts justly He is not doing so

---

5. "14. God Is Love," para. 14.

6. Pink, *Attributes of God*, 81.

7. Tozer, *Knowledge of the Holy*, 98.

8. Tozer, *Knowledge of the Holy*, 102

to conform to an independent criterion, but simply acting like Himself in a given situation.[9]

We are yet again brought to the cross. Here God's wrath and justice are directed at sin. We must always be thankful for the cross, and it should motivate us to bring the message of the cross to those under condemnation. The pain of the social issues we face in the world cannot even be compared to the pain of eternal punishment faced by those who do not know God through Jesus Christ. (John 3:18) Having been made in the image of God (*imago Dei*) and having been adopted into his family, we have a sense of righteousness within us. One of the ways God reveals himself to us is in our conscience. We long for justice, and we know when we have acted unjustly. "That's not fair!" is heard on the playground from the earliest of ages.

We must see the difference between God's justice and the injustices in the world. We must imitate God in justice. How do we respond when we see injustice in the world? We must live missionally, like the good Samaritan, especially when we witness injustice around us (Isa 1:17; Jas 1:27). God has told us what this should mean to us:

> He has shown you, O mortal, what is good. And what does the LORD require of you? To act justly and to love mercy and to walk humbly with your God. (Mic 6:8)

Clearly, our ministry strategies should include acts of kindness and attempts to bring about justice in a broken world.

God's Transcendence in a Fearful World

A third attribute that must be included in the discussion of seeking God's heart for the lost is his transcendence. Unless we see him as being above all, we will be timid in our attempts to bless others. Knowing that God is near enables us to face our fears of offending others, of being rejected, or of doing it all wrong. "'Am I only a God nearby,' declares the Lord, 'and not a God far away?'" (Jer 23:23–24). How can we comprehend the nearness of an infinite God?

> When we speak of God as transcendent we mean of course that He is exalted far above the created universe, so far above that human thought cannot imagine it. To think accurately about this, however, we must keep in mind that 'far above' does not here refer to physical distance from the earth but to quality of

---

9. Tozer, *Knowledge of the Holy*, 87.

being. We are concerned not with location in space nor with mere altitude, but with life.[10]

> For this is what the high and exalted One says—he who lives forever, whose name is holy: 'I live in a high and holy place, but also with the one who is contrite and lowly in spirit, to revive the heart of the contrite.' (Isa 57:15)

When we encounter God, to the extent that we comprehend him in all his glory and transcendence, we will fall before him in awe and reverence. This holy dread leads to doing his will. But the dread must come first! We seem to have lost this in our casual treatment of God. Only when we truly see God will we also see the spiritual needs of others. Our response is to do what he calls us to do to reflect his love and justice to others. And what we do must be done to bring glory to his name.

LOVING OTHERS AS MEANS TO GLORIFY GOD

You see, one of our temptations is doing good deeds for others but with selfish motives. In chapter 1, I wrote about the pin-the-call-on-the-map activity I use in class. Students blindly put arrows on a map in a mock exercise to determine God's sovereign call upon their lives. After the arrows are placed on the map, I let them know that each arrow has landed where there is need, for there are needs everywhere. The point, again, is not that of finding need but of discerning how the Lord may be leading. When you first arrive in the field, it is easy to feel inundated with the needs all around you. Unless you are calloused to the felt needs, you will want to help in whatever ways you can. But choices must be made. Before those choices happen, however, it helps to examine your heart.

Recently, our daughter and son-in-law, serving in Thailand, sent out a prayer letter. Here is an excerpt from it:

> To be a missionary is to daily acknowledge that much of the world is desperately lost and in need of reconciliation with God. There are days when that knowledge is crushing. The temptation is to become either hardhearted or brokenhearted. A hardened heart lacks compassion, and a broken heart lacks hope. We're called to live in the tension with a tender heart (1 Pet 3:8), but who can do that on their own? How do you daily decide to care, but not be overwhelmed?

10. Tozer, *Knowledge of the Holy*, 69.

This past week, Rob Foster, the speaker at the international church that we attend, told about his daughter asking, 'How do I guard my heart without having a hard heart?' He told her the only answer is to give your heart to Jesus every day. That's where we long to be, with our hearts tenderly held by Jesus as we acknowledge that the world hurts all over and still take our small steps of obedience toward bringing His light where there is only darkness.[11]

She raises an important issue. We must ask ourselves if all of our virtuous acts are truly virtuous or not. By examining our hearts, we can better serve others in a way that glorifies God. Let me be honest with you. I struggle at times with this. In Gary Chapman's book, *The 5 Love Languages: The Secret to Love that Lasts*, he describes how we tend to prefer different manners of love: words of affirmation, quality time, receiving gifts, acts of service, or physical touch. Personally, I connect strongly with words of affirmation and physical touch. Regarding words of affirmation, I sometimes need to guard myself against serving others in order to get the appreciation and admiration of others.

What is our motivation for loving others or fighting injustice? Is it to give in order to get? Is it to feel good about ourselves? Is it to alleviate pain and suffering? Or is it to reflect God's heart, a heart that loves others to bring glory to himself? Do we hate injustice because of how people suffer or because it reflects a broken creation, not the way God intended it to be? We must guard against being guided solely by our emotions, as that can cloud the deeper purpose of all we do—to bring glory to the Creator God.

Jesus Modeled the Ministry of Compassionate Presence

This is not to imply that we should not be compassionate. Jesus modeled compassion throughout his time on Earth. Like Jesus, we need to recognize that physical needs and spiritual needs are interconnected. In my years of living overseas, I have seen hundreds of opportunities to minister to others. It is heartbreaking to see the effects of sin on the people of this world. I thank the Lord for the many who follow the Lord's leading to care for the downtrodden and destitute.

Early this week, I got another ministry update from someone serving in the Isaan area of Thailand. She wrote,

---

11. Kara Hallead, personal communication, August 24, 2019.

God broke our hearts last week as we returned to Ubon to serve food to over 600 people who are homeless due to the severe flooding. When we got out of the car, I had several grandma's hanging off of me, sobbing and thanking us for worrying and bringing food. It started to rain when we were there, and one little girl came running over and asked if I would hold her because she was afraid more flooding would come.[12]

The team's continued presence in this part of the world is a big part of their love for the people. Adding tangible help (in this case, food) only serves to strengthen the bond between them.

She goes on to write,

God has blessed me in so many ways and above and beyond my wildest thoughts with the people He's placed in my life. He has given me more grandma's and Aunties then I sometimes know what to do with. It's cultural in Thailand to address someone as grandma, mom, auntie, uncle, dad, grandpa, etc here before using their name, but occasionally God places people in my life who truly become family. God has truly blessed me by giving me a Thai mom who calls me, encourages me and prays for me daily. Please be praying for Mom Nang as she's been having heart problems lately. I'm not sure if it's due to stress or if there is something more. This past Sunday, she sobbed on me saying she needs to go to the doctor but is so scared as to what he might find. Pray for wisdom for the doctors and great strength and trust in Jesus for her (she's an incredible believer).[13]

Loving people is both rewarding and hard. Please be praying for (my teammates) and I as we love (too deeply it feels at times) the people around us. Pray for continued wisdom in explaining Jesus and their need for a Savior. Pray for ways to explain what sin is (as most Buddhists think they haven't sinned in years). Pray we'd know how to love those who frustrate or disappoint us.[14]

As stated in that last sentence, loving others is not always enjoyable. If we are doing it to get something in return, we will be disappointed. It can be difficult to not receive any thanks for blessing others. At times like those, we need to push back feelings of arrogance ("Why aren't they more thankful for me?" "Don't they know what I gave up to be here?").

12. Erin Seppanan, personal communication, September 26, 2019.

13. Erin Seppanan, personal communication, September 26, 2019.

14. Erin Seppanan, personal communication, September 26, 2019.

God is aware and able. He is aware of the needs around you, and he is able to meet those needs. What is your role? Having sought his mind and asked for wisdom to know what to pursue, may you also seek his loving heart as you seek to address the needs of a broken world around you. But may you do so for his glory and not just an emotional response. His love, justice, and transcendence combine to point us to our unique contributions to restoring broken people to himself.

QUESTIONS

1. What types of needs pull at your heart? How does this reflect your personality or your understanding of God?

2. As you look around you today, are there needs that you can meet? What would keep you from doing so?

3. Related to meeting needs, what temptations do you face regarding motivations apart from seeking to bring glory to God?

4. What other attributes of God come to bear on choosing your ministry strategy?

Chapter 10

Church Planting

God Is All-powerful, so We Must Trust Him to Build His Church

"And on this rock I will build My church, and the gates of Hades will not overcome it." (Matt 16:18)

"The church is called to lead a life such that it is both an announcement and a foretaste of the reign of God."

—JUSTO GONZÁLEZ[1]

ONE OF MY STRONGEST memories of the churches in Thailand is how they responded during the aftermath of the massive tsunami that hit southern Thailand (as well as Indonesia and Sri Lanka) in 2004. As I was involved in a ministry that focused on caring for cross-cultural workers, I knew many caregivers, both Thai and expatriate, who went down to help. And the local churches gave supplies to help with the efforts for a long time after the tragedy. This was the church in action.

Somebody very dear to me shared why his friends and he have grown dissatisfied with the church. It boils down to a perception of the church's unwillingness to respond to the needs around them. According to them, the

1. González, *Knowing Our Faith*, 87.

evangelical church has turned its back on the poor, abused, and marginalized. Unfortunately, there is a decent amount of truth in this perception. However, the problem with that perception is that it is tunnel-focused, ignoring all the many ways the church is a blessing to the world. As has been said in the past and is still true today, the local church is the hope of the world.

A quick study of how the church has positively impacted society around the world yields the following: healthcare, education, women's status being raised, rescuing from trafficking, and so much more. Now has the church also been on the wrong side of some issues? Absolutely. But to accuse the church of being heartless is misleading at best. It would be like saying that any organization is characterized by its worst representation, rather than by its best.

When functioning as intended, according to the Bible, the church is God's hand for positive transformation in the world he desperately loves. So it stands to reason that church planting needs to be done well. As the Chinese saying goes, "A journey of a thousand (miles) begins with a single step."

PLANTING THE FIRST CHURCH—
OVERCOMING INERTIA

When I first arrived in China, as mentioned in chapter 1, I was often asked personal questions. I had to learn a new set of privacy guidelines. But I also needed to learn how to help them to put me in a box. Those I met wanted to know who I am to them. My identity was that I was an English teacher. But this was just the first step to establishing myself in the community. Being part of the community is essential to building trust. As trust is built, opportunities to share God's word present themselves. Eventually, individuals come to Christ. The time has now come to gather the new believers together. This is when the church begins.

Let me be clear about what constitutes a church. This is sometimes a point of contention. And many books have been written about ecclesiology. My intent here is to keep it simple and scriptural. While I am not an advocate for building theology on the book of Acts, I believe that Acts 2:42–47 gives a good start to citing some of the characteristics of a church:

> They devoted themselves to the apostles' teaching and to fellowship, to the breaking of bread and to prayer. Everyone was filled with awe at the many wonders and signs performed by the apostles. All the believers were together and had everything in common. They sold property and possessions to give to anyone who had need. Every day they continued to meet together in the

temple courts. They broke bread in their homes and ate together with glad and sincere hearts, praising God and enjoying the favor of all the people. And the Lord added to their number daily those who were being saved.

Getting started with the first church in a new ministry setting is something that requires much intentionality, patience, and humility. The concept of *church* comes from the Greek word *ekklesia* (literally, called out ones). The church in Acts 2 demonstrates that a church is a group of believers who are called out to be communally devoted to the following: fellowship with one another, studying the teachings of the apostles, remembering the Lord's table, praying, and caring for each other. As they maintained these commitments, "the Lord added to their number daily those who were being saved."

The Physics of Church Planting

In my Biblical Theology of Missions class, we discuss the physics of church. I utilize the following terms related to force to describe churches: centripetalism, centrifugalism, inertia, and friction. All churches will exhibit or encounter all four forces with a propensity towards one. Those churches that lean more centripetally will have a focus on internal attraction. Like a whirlpool, the idea is to have a "come and see" approach. These churches will seek to be attractive to those outside the church. In the above Acts 2 passage, many came to faith, at least in part, it seems, because of what they saw happening in the church. Growth of the believers resulted in an increase of believers. The challenge to this approach is that the church can lose sight of the world around them as they center their efforts on themselves.

The second force exhibited by churches is centrifugal. These are those that view their mission with a "go-and-tell" emphasis. Not content to be attractive, like those holding on to a merry-go-round, they feel cast out to those who might never enter a church, both locally and globally. "But you will receive power when the Holy Spirit comes on you; and you will be my witnesses in Jerusalem, and in all Judea and Samaria, and to the ends of the earth" (Acts 1:8). Notice the necessity of receiving God's power for this to happen.

> In any case, one must stress the fact that mission is always turned outwards. Although the inner life of the church is part of its mission as a sign of hope for the world, it is not a matter of having a sacred corner where we can withdraw from the difficulties of the world in order to rejoice in our mutual love. Instead, it's a matter of having this experience of Christian life move us in two

parallel directions. The first of these is witness to the Lord of the church. The second is to discover, acknowledge, and point out the presence of that very Lord in other places around us.[2]

It is important that we stop here for a moment and remind ourselves that this is not an either/or proposition. Rather, it should be a both/and scenario. And it also is not a good/bad choice to be made. Each church and, for that matter, each individual, must decide how the Lord is leading. Evangelism and discipleship do not happen passively. For the other two forces, inertia and friction, are those that work against both centripetal and centrifugal strategies of reaching others. Inertia is that which keeps one from getting up and doing something in the first place. As Newton's first law of motion states, a body at rest remains at rest until an external force acts upon it. In other words, it is easier to continue to do nothing than to start to do something. Likewise, friction is any force that would hinder or slow down movement. In the case of reaching out to others, this could be in the form of spiritual warfare, relational conflict, finances, etc.

LEANING ON GOD'S POWER— "I WILL BUILD MY CHURCH"

Many sending agencies have church planting as one of their core values. We do well to remember that it is God who plants churches and initiates church-planting movements. This is why it is imperative to lean on God's omnipotence, his being all-powerful, when attempting to see a church planted among all people groups around the world. Our response will then be one of amazement at what God is doing. On the other hand, when we fail to recognize God's role in seeing churches planted, we will tend to see success as our own doing. We get pulled into prideful thoughts such as, "Look at what I've done." Or, "God sure must be pleased with me." This is a dangerous path, as it robs God of his glory. It is *his* church, and *he* is the One who builds it.

God is all-powerful, so we must trust him to build his church. It is a spiritual battle; otherwise, Jesus would not have said, "and the gates of Hades will not overcome it" (Matt 16:18). Omnipotence speaks to God's ability to do whatever he wants. His love and sovereignty speak to God's reasoning to do whatever brings him the most glory. His omnipotence and sovereignty combine to establish his authority, especially when referring to the Great Commission (Matt 28:18–20).

2. González, *Knowing Our Faith*, 96.

But too often we forget the word 'therefore,' which implies that the reason why Jesus is telling this to his disciples has just been mentioned. Certainly, we are to go and make disciples. But the reason for this is not that we are take Jesus to places where he is not present. On the contrary, the reason for our mission is that Jesus is already Lord of all nations.[3]

From the very beginning of time, when God created out of nothing (Gen 1), his power has been on display. "By the word of the LORD the heavens were made" (Ps 33:6). This is especially seen in the outworking of his purposes to bring glory to himself and to draw those created in his image back to a relationship with him. And, as Job pointed out, "I know that you can do all things; no purpose of yours can be thwarted" (Job 42:2).

While on earth, Jesus demonstrated this same omnipotence on several occasions. From the feeding of the 5,000, walking on water, and healing many (Mark 6:30–56) to raising Lazarus from the dead (John 11:38–44), Jesus lived out what he said in Matthew 19:26: "with God all things are possible."

This same power is at work in our lives today. The task of church planting can be daunting. We must not try to do it in our own strength. We depend on him and his power as we trust him to bless our efforts to accomplish his desire of the church being built. And we do so without fear as we move forward in confidence. "The Lord is the strength of my life; of whom shall I be afraid?" (Ps 27:1).

RESPONDING TO GOD'S POWER—"WHAT MUST I DO?"

In Acts 16, Paul and Silas were causing a stir in Philippi, especially after Paul's casting out a demon from a fortune-teller. Being put into the deep recesses of the prison, Paul and Silas prayed and sang hymns. Then God miraculously used an earthquake to shake the prison and then caused the doors to fly open and the chains to come loose:

> The jailer woke up, and when he saw the prison doors open, he drew his sword and was about to kill himself because he thought the prisoners had escaped. But Paul shouted, "Don't harm yourself! We are all here!" The jailer called for lights, rushed in and fell trembling before Paul and Silas. He then brought them out and asked, "Sirs, what must I do to be saved?" (Acts 16:27–30)

---

3. González, *Knowing Our Faith*, 98.

I had long been amazed at how the jailer's first question was about salvation and not about what happened in the natural world. But the more I pondered this, the more I realized that his question was a response to what he saw and heard from and about Paul and Silas. In other words, what we do and say, along with what our powerful God does in our presence, will determine what questions we are asked. This, then, is the beginning of ministry. We need to live our lives before men in such a way that they ask us about the God we worship. This is especially true in societies where they live under a fear/power paradigm. Their fear of the evil spirits, for example, is alleviated when they encounter the all-powerful God.

And just as the jailer was concerned for his household (in Greek, *oikos*) and not just for himself, we must recognize that a majority of the world live in community-based societies. An individualistic approach will not work in these places. Church planting in communities is about building communities of Christ-followers that bless their communities. Again, this is not something that can be done apart from a work of God. To think that we can affect this kind of change is arrogance.

For a church to be planted, there first must be believers. How do we share the gospel in a cross-cultural context? At the risk of oversimplifying things (I teach an entire semester's course on cross-cultural communication, based in part on David Hesselgrave's classic, *Communicating Christ Cross-culturally*), we need to build bridges of understanding and acceptance.

This inevitably leads to the topic of contextualization. How do we make the gospel message understandable in the local culture and language without compromising Scripture or promoting syncretism? Don Richardson has written extensively about redemptive analogies, ways to use artifacts or customs in the local culture to connect with the gospel. His book, *Peace Child*, presents a clear example of how this created a breakthrough moment for his ministry among the Sawi. At one point, he was growing frustrated at not finding a way to help the Sawi understand the gospel message. And when the tribal fighting got to be too much, he threatened to leave if the fighting did not stop. When it abruptly stopped, he learned that the tribes had instituted the Peace Child practice of swapping infants. As long as each peace child lived, there would be peace between the tribes. Richardson could now tell them about God's Peace Child, Jesus Christ. The breakthrough was amazing.

Similar questions relate to how new believers should congregate. Much discussion has taken place about what the church should look like. Should it be a house or cell church, a storefront church, a dedicated building like a community center, a megachurch, or some other structure? And how do the local culture and the local politics impact how public the church should be?

Recently, Brian DeVries[4] wrote about six different contexts for contextualization: incarnational contextualization (how much the cross-cultural worker "becomes as" the locals in culture), missional contextualization (how the gospel message is made understandable and acceptable), ecclesial contextualization (what local church and worship looks like), reformational contextualization (how the new church lives out its faith), reflectional contextualization (how the cross-cultural worker changes throughout his ministry experience), and global contextualization (how churches, both sending and local, grow in their understanding that they are part of something bigger than themselves). This raises the bar on the contextualization discussion in a very helpful manner.

First Steps in Planting a Church

When we arrived in China, it wasn't long before we saw God's power at work in the lives of our students. As some came to faith in Jesus Christ, we began Bible studies in our apartment. We were very careful, knowing that doing so in a Communist country was risky. Even after our first bathtub baptisms, we felt the Lord's leading to continue without fear.

Because we continued at the same university for nearly seven years, we became some of the few who remained constant where we were. As a result, it was not unusual to have other cross-cultural workers come to us and share the good news that one of their students or friends had come to Christ. Unfortunately, because the workers' time was ending, they were returning to their passport countries. They were asking us to add their disciple to our Bible study and discipleship ministry. We never declined such a request. But with a growing ministry, it also had the potential to become more visible to those who would potentially seek to hinder what God was doing.

A Chinese house church pastor and his wife were among those that were put in touch with us. We gladly mentored them in ministry and family life. It was a blessing to have them join the group. Yang and Zhou (not their real names) became invaluable to us. Yang would join me on visits to different cities to connect with some of our disciples who had graduated and moved back to their hometowns. I felt like we were Paul and Silas encouraging those in the faith. And Carol and Zhou developed a precious relationship that continues to this day.

And then one day, Yang came to me and said that he was sensing from the Holy Spirit that we should temporarily discontinue our Bible studies with the group. My confidence in Yang's ability to hear from God was

4. DeVries, "Contexts of Contextualization," 11–14.

complete. We stopped. A couple of weeks later, I was approached by a student on behalf of the university's Communist Party Secretary. This student and I had a strong level of trust with each other, and I appreciated that it was him that was sent to me. He was tasked with asking me if I was holding Christian activities in my home. Thanks to Yang's listening to the Lord and our subsequent discontinuing of our Bible studies, I could honestly reply, "We are not at this time holding any Christian activities in our home." I think my student understood what I was saying and could, with integrity, report back what I said.

Is God powerful enough to orchestrate such occurrences? Absolutely! And imagine how everyone in the discipleship ministry responded to seeing the Lord enter into our lives in such a personal and powerful way. The history of the church is replete with examples of God demonstrating his power in such a way that resulted in "the Lord (adding) to their number daily those who were being saved." All glory to God!

> Now to him who is able to do immeasurably more than all we
> ask or imagine, according to his power that is at work within us,
> to him be glory in the church and in Christ Jesus throughout all
> generations, for ever and ever! Amen. (Eph 3:20–21)

QUESTIONS

1. How have your past and present church experiences shaped your view of the church?

2. Make a list of all the ways that the local church can positively impact your community.

3. When have you seen God's power at work in your life and in the lives of those around you?

4. How might your ministry be impacted by displays of God's power? Take these to the Lord in prayer.

Chapter 11

Empowering Church Multiplication

God Is Infinite, so We Can Relax Our Control and Watch the Church Multiply

"My prayer is not for them alone. I pray also for those who will believe in Me through their message." (John 17:20)

"We need to be talking about multiplication everywhere if we want multiplication everywhere."

—ED STETZER[1]

RECENTLY, THE LANCASTER BIBLE College Women's Volleyball team won two five-set matches in a row. When our daughter, who had played on the team in her time at LBC, heard about this, her first comment was about how that requires great conditioning. She understands that conditioning makes it possible to maintain endurance throughout a long battle. The thing about conditioning is that it necessarily starts on the first day of practice and is never ignored throughout the season. And so it is with church planting. It is a long-term proposition that requires discipline and a long-term commitment. The goal is beyond human resourcing, so we lean on an infinite God to see his church multiplied around the world.

1. Stetzer, "Church Planting Series: Creating a Culture of Multiplication," para. 14.

In my Discipleship/Evangelism class, we begin by discussing when discipleship begins. While some posit that it begins at the moment of conversion, we quickly come to a consensus that it begins the moment you meet somebody. In the conversation, we include the Engel scale which provides a helpful visual of the different stages a person works through in her spiritual journey. Negative numbers represent how far a person is from believing in Jesus Christ as Savior. The value of zero represents the point of conversion. And positive numbers represent the increasingly close relationship a believer has with God. At the initial meeting with someone, the Christian should ask the Lord to show her where the other person is on the scale in order to better know how to help that person come to an understanding and acceptance of Christ. So that first meeting becomes a starting point for discipleship. And, as people come to Christ, getting them into fellowship with other believers is critical for their long-term spiritual development.

In China, as students came to Christ, Carol and I realized that we needed to get our new believers into church as part of the discipleship and church-planting processes. We quickly became educated in the Chinese church situation. In China, there are two types of churches, the government-sanctioned Three Self Patriotic Movement (TSPM) churches and the nongovernment-sanctioned churches (mostly underground house churches). The three principles are self-supporting (not relying on outside funds), self-governing, and self-propagating. These were developed by the Chinese government as an attempt to eliminate what was perceived as imperial influence from missionaries coming into China.

A common error made by foreign Christians serving in China is to assume that all TSPM churches are bad and full of false teaching or that all house churches are vibrant and Bible-centered. It is not that easy a distinction to make. With the help of Yang and Zhou, we learned which TSPM churches in our city were good options for our disciples and which house church we could connect others to.

One of the reasons for this assumption is that many cross-cultural workers struggle to remember that the Holy Spirit that called and empowered them into ministry is the same Holy Spirit that resides in the new believers and local churches. This may be an indication of how difficult it is to release control. But focusing on how God is infinite helps us to see how he has a perspective that we do not have. This, in turn, will help us to see his long-term desire of seeing multiplying churches.

TAKING A LONG-TERM APPROACH—
THE ALPHA AND THE OMEGA

Since God is infinite, his goals, plans, and desires never change. The purpose of the church remains to glorify him and to make him known. This is best done through churches that live out who God is and through multiplying themselves in churches that do the same. When combined with his being immutable, God's being infinite challenges us to see our misguided attempts to manipulate something of eternal consequences (Ps 103:17–19).

One church-planting movement that I have been blessed to observe has been in central Cambodia. Our team arrived there in 1998 and took on the long-term process of learning the language and culture before arriving in a central province to begin their ministry in a small town. As local Khmer came to Christ, a house church was started. From the beginning, they imparted the values of the church's role in the community and its responsibility to reproduce itself. Today, there are nine churches in the province, representing three generations of church plants from that original church.

Recently, I interviewed the team leaders to get their thoughts on how they instilled the value of being a reproducing church in that first church plant. One thing they said was that the team believed that they were planting the church of fifty years from now when they started. In other words, it was an eternal mindset, one that looked far into the future and not just at the present. This reflects God's being eternal and infinite (Rev 1:8; Isa 40:28; Deut 33:27; Ps 48:14).

Yes, he will guide us, but we need to listen to and follow his guidance. We get so impatient at times that we make decisions based on immediate gratification or short-sighted gains (Pss 90:1–4; 100:5). "But do not overlook this one fact, beloved, that with the Lord one day is as a thousand years, and a thousand years as one day" (2 Pet 3:8).

God's being infinite means that his attributes have no limits. God is the *El Olam* (literally, "the Everlasting/Perpetual God"). Our church-planting strategies need to incorporate this aspect of God. The best way to do this is to prioritize discipleship and church multiplication. As we follow the Lord's leading and watch him work, we get to see impact that will last long after we are gone.

In John 15, Jesus uses the vine to talk about the importance of a close relationship with him. But he also clearly communicates the importance of generational growth as the progression goes from bearing fruit (v. 5) to bearing much fruit (8) to bearing fruit that will remain (16). The importance of what we do being both long-lasting and reproducible can easily be lived out through church-planting movements.

CHURCH MULTIPLICATION—
FRUIT THAT WILL REMAIN

Recently, in *Christianity Today*, Ed Stetzer wrote a five-part series on church planting. In the first article,[2] he addresses fears and concerns that many churches have related to planting churches. Among other things, he cites how many churches never establish a culture of multiplication. This is sometimes coupled with a lack of kingdom vision, focusing too much on inward growth. He goes on, in subsequent installments, to present principles to be followed in church multiplication. One of those is that "Church planting is always a sacrifice."[3] Perhaps this is partially why it does not happen as often as it should. But one of the best takeaways from all of these articles is Stetzer's emphasis on discipleship. This is how multiplication takes place, first at the individual level and then at the congregational level.

The church-planting movement in Cambodia was begun with an emphasis on life-on-life discipleship and leadership development. Along with teaching the new believers to be self-feeders from the word, the first church was taught to plant another church as soon as possible. The concept was that nobody should have to go to a church further than they can easily get to, whether by walking or a short motorcycle ride. This made the church outward-focused from the beginning.

Leadership development came in two forms. First, it came from personal discipleship from the cross-cultural workers there. And it also came by connecting the potential leaders with local Khmer church leaders who have been committed to the upcoming leaders through seminars and personal mentoring. This dual-impact approach helped the young church leaders to see that Christianity is not just a Western religion. But it also quickly reduced dependency on the cross-cultural workers. So today, the team that helped to start the ministry there have all left and only have periodic communication with the Khmer churches.

Dependency is a danger faced by many infant church-planting movements. The cross-cultural workers, as mentioned earlier, sometimes struggle to trust that the Holy Spirit that led them to their place of ministry is also at work in the new believers and infant church. We sometimes have the mentality that we cannot hand over the responsibility of the church until leaders are developed. Rather, we should recognize that, inasmuch as it possible, it is theirs from the beginning.

---

2. Stetzer, "Church Planting Series: Creating a Culture of Multiplication," paras. 6–8

3. Stetzer, "Church Planting Series: How Can Your Church Get Involved in Church Planting?," para. 20.

In *Passing the Baton*, Tom Steffen[4] writes about the stages of disengagement that the cross-cultural worker moves through. From the very beginning, an exit strategy (phase out) needs to be in place. The cross-cultural worker moves from being more parental to becoming a consultant and then cheerleader. As Paul and Silas purposed to go back to encourage churches that were earlier planted, churches should be allowed to thrive on their own without feeling as though they have been abandoned.

One specific area of reproducibility that should be considered is the use of technology. I remember visiting a relatively young church in rural northeast Thailand. The ministry that started this church helped them to have many of the Western tools of worship, including the instruments "needed" for a worship band, as well as a computer and projector for their PowerPoint presentations. One highly significant problem with this is that it was not reproducible in any potential church plants from that first church. It grew a dependency on outside funds. And equally concerning was the suggestion that the worship service should be Western in nature, rather than something more indigenous to the local culture.

This again brings us to the contextualization question. How indigenous should the local church of new believers be? A guiding principle should be related to how small can we keep the gap of understanding and acceptance for those in the local culture. For example, why should new believers have to learn another language to worship God? And why not incorporate biblically permissible forms of the local culture into their worship? On the other end of the spectrum, we need to guard against syncretism, when there appears to be no difference between the believer and the nonbeliever. There has been much debate about insider movements, where new believers continue in their former religious context as secret believers in order to potentially bring others to faith. One of the concerns with this is with the level of deception that could lead to a loss of integrity.

Long-term Impact Necessitates Leadership Development

Integrity is just one area that needs to be protected and cultivated. Another is how the Bible is understood. Sending agencies concerned with the level of biblical understanding by those they send out require adequate Bible training. This is wise. And perhaps the most important training comes in the area of hermeneutics, knowing how to accurately understand and interpret the Scriptures. This same concern should be shared by those training new believers and rising leaders.

4. Steffen, *Passing the Baton*, 5–7.

One potential challenge faced by many is the mode of biblical education. Some elect to send those that they perceive to be potential church leaders to Bible colleges in the city or to another country. While this may prove helpful for their education, it results in some challenges. For example, some never come back. They find that there are attractive opportunities in the city (or another country) that they never would have had in their home village or town. And even if they do come back, they have changed. They do not always easily reenter their home context. These challenges need to be weighed against the benefit of a formal Bible education.

A way to mitigate the challenges of sending rising leaders away for formal Bible education is to develop a leadership development strategy that includes personal mentoring and discipleship. This seems to be Paul's thinking when he wrote in 2 Timothy 2:2: "And the things you have heard me say in the presence of many witnesses entrust to reliable men who will also be qualified to teach others."

Multiplication, Not Addition

In his classic book on discipleship, *Disciples Are Made Not Born: Helping Others Grow to Maturity in Christ*, Walter Henrichsen writes,

> This is a multiplicative process. While the faithful men are teaching others also, Timothy is in the process of raising up more faithful men, who shall be able to teach others also. Implementing this vision of multiplying disciples constitutes the only way Christ's commission can ever ultimately be fulfilled. Other ministries and approaches can augment it but never replace it.[5]

Many examples of the effectiveness of multiplication versus addition have been developed. Let me share two of them. The first is the grain on a chessboard illustration. A chessboard is made up of sixty-four squares. If you put one grain of wheat on the first square and then double it each square (two on the second, four on the third, eight on the fourth, etc.), on (just) the sixty-fourth square, there would be 18,446,744,073,551,615 grains of wheat (about 1.2 million TONS!!!).

To contrast addition and multiplication in terms of reproducing disciples, we can look at simple mathematics. On the addition side, let us make a bold assumption that ten gifted evangelists lead 1,000 people to the Lord each year. At the end of the first year, there will be 10,000 converts.

---

5. Henrichsen, *Disciples Are Made Not Born*, 11.

Assuming continual similar acts of God, after thirty years, there would be 300,000 converts to Christ.

But if we instead focus on discipleship, let us look at the impact of disciple-makers reproducing themselves. If ten Christians pour themselves each into one person in such a way that at the end of the year, they are able to do the same to others, we will have twenty disciple-makers. If these twenty, during the second year, each do the same again, there will be forty disciple-makers at the end of the second year. If this process were to continue for the same thirty years that saw 300,000 converts to Christ through the addition process, there would be more than 10 billion disciple-makers!

Naturally, these are hypothetical. The logic of the exercise eventually breaks down. For one thing, we need to realize that, at some point in time, jumps of geography will need to take place. This, by the way, is strong evidence for the need for cross-cultural ministry. We need to be going to the places where there is no gospel light. But nonetheless, the lesson is clear. God's plan of discipleship is effective, and it is doable.

It is doable because God is infinite. His being infinite means that he is always available and able to engage and empower those who enter the discipleship process. It is also doable because every believer can be involved in discipleship. As a reminder, Jesus said, "My prayer is not for them alone. I pray also for those who will believe in Me through their message" (John 17:20).

QUESTIONS

1. How have you benefited (or not) from others' investing in your spiritual journey?

2. Who in your life could you pour into to help them grow in their walk with the Lord?

3. What excuses have you used in the past to keep you from discipling someone else?

4. How does the knowledge that God is infinite impact those excuses?

PART 4

Return

Chapter 12

Leaving the Field

God is Good and Immanent, so We Can Trust Him
When It's Time to Say Good-bye to the Ministry,
Whether Temporarily or Permanently

"Now I commit you to God and to the word of His grace, which can build you up and give you an inheritance among all those who are sanctified." (Acts 20:32)

"The goodness of God is the life of the believer's trust."

—ARTHUR PINK[1]

"But what if I don't come back?"

I remember when we were getting ready to go back to the USA for our first time after arriving in China. When we attended another agency's retreat, on our way into China, I heard many stories of those who never came back from their first Home Assignment (furlough). I allowed this fear to grow in my heart. Looking back on this time, more than thirty years ago, I can see how silly it was. But it was real to me back then.

When the time finally did come for us to leave southeast Asia, after serving there for twenty-three years, it was nothing short of traumatic. The fact that it happened in a short period of time made it more difficult than

---

1. Pink, *Attributes of God*, 60.

it needed to be. The Lord, having called us to serve him in this part of the world, blessed us with an equally confirming call back to the USA. Having completed my doctorate in missiology two years earlier, I had shared with a friend my desire to (sometime in the future) move into either a missions pastor role or to teach at a Christian university. When I received an email from that same friend, who was now part of a search committee for Lancaster Bible College (LBC), Carol and I had mixed feelings. On the one hand, we were excited about the opportunity of leading the intercultural studies program at LBC. This would be a great way to pour into the next generation of cross-cultural workers. On the other hand, it would be very difficult to say good-bye to the many close relationships we had in Asia and around the world.

The hiring process went in spurts and sputters for several reasons. At one point toward the end of it, we were leading a retreat of all of our team leaders and their families. This led into a retreat for all the workers serving in our area. This would provide a great opportunity for us to share how the Lord was moving. As we waited for confirmation from LBC, we found ourselves walking gingerly between saying too much too soon and not saying enough. As it turned out, we got the confirmation in time to share with the leadership the last day of their retreat—on April 1. As we shared the news, some thought we were playing an April Fool's joke on them. We weren't. And so began the process of transitioning and leaving.

As I wrote in chapter 4, good-byes are hard. And that's not a bad thing in itself. The apostle Paul experienced this pain as well. In Acts 20, we read the account of his saying good-bye to the church in Ephesus. I use this passage with my graduating seniors each semester. Carol and I also used it with our team leaders when we were preparing to say good-bye to them at the end of our missionary service. Paul concludes his farewell speech with a statement of entrusting them to God: "Now I commit you to God and to the word of His grace, which can build you up and give you an inheritance among all those who are sanctified" (Acts 20:32).

In times of loss and transition, we lean heavily on the goodness of God and his immanence, the knowledge that he is near. Our responses to these attributes of God in times of transition are those of contentment, satisfaction and trust. If we fail to lean on God, we will open ourselves up to various fears.

GOD IS GOOD ALL THE TIME; AND ALL THE TIME, GOD IS GOOD.

I often hear this sentence thrown around in Christian circles. My concern is not with the truth of the statement, because it is true that God is good all the time and that, all the time, God is good. However, as with many such statements, it seems to have lost some of its impact because of how easily it is used. When we lost a daughter to a premature birth in Thailand, it really was remembering God's goodness that helped us through the grieving of the loss of Hope Ann. Grieving is a good thing, but it is hard. Leaning on the goodness of God makes it bearable.

But what does it mean to say that God is good? As with all of God's attributes, we need to turn to Scripture to see how it is described and how it is to impact us. Even from the beginning, when God created all things, we read that God saw what he had done and said that "it was good." (Gen 1). One easily observable trait about God's goodness is that it has an object. That is, being good is best revealed in actions towards others. This is not to say that the object of goodness is more important that the giver of good things. Rather, receiving acts of goodness point to the quality of the good giver (Ps 145:9; Matt 7:11; Mark 10:18; 1 Chr 16:34) "Oh, taste and see that the LORD is good! Blessed is the man who takes refuge in him" (Ps 34:8).

These verses begin to point us in the direction of how we are to respond to God's goodness. First, we give thanks. Knowing the goodness of God makes it possible for us to give thanks even in times of loss and sorrow, including saying good-bye to those we love. "Let them thank the LORD for his steadfast love, for his wondrous works to the children of man! For he satisfies the longing soul, and the hungry soul he fills with good things" (Ps 107:8–9).

Secondly, we are to take refuge in God. Knowing that God is good comforts us as we come into his presence. The story of Joseph reveals God's goodness throughout his sovereign orchestration of Joseph's life. When Joseph finally reveals himself to his brothers, he comforts them by saying, "As for you, you meant evil against me, but God meant it for good, to bring it about that many people should be kept alive" (Gen 50:20).

Another response to God's goodness is a growing desire to be led by this good God. "You are good and do good; teach me your statutes" (Ps 119:68). He will surely answer this prayer:

> And I am sure of this, that he who began a good work in you will bring it to completion at the day of Jesus Christ." (Phil 1:6)

Finally, our resting in God's goodness should also lead us to accept what he brings our way and act accordingly (1 Tim 4:4; Rom 12:1–2).

In my days as a philosophy major, a common discussion topic was how a good God could allow evil in the world. This is sometimes an attempt to discredit God. However, the existence of evil in the world points to God's goodness. Evil in the world does not mean that God is not good. The desire for "Thy kingdom come, Thy will be done on earth as it is in heaven" (Matt 6:10) is an expression of a desire for good to be reestablished here on earth. Pain, including saying good-bye, is not an indication of badness. A theology of suffering must include a discussion of the goodness of pain. "The LORD is good, a stronghold in the day of trouble; he knows those who take refuge in him" (Nah 1:7).

Combined with a few of his other attributes, God is infinitely, completely, and permanently good. He is the *summum bonum*, the chiefest good. So he is a rock to stand on in times of transition. "The goodness of God is the life of the believer's trust."[2]

THE GOOD IN GOOD-BYES

Good-byes rarely feel good. If they do, then there is another issue involved. But saying good-bye to those we have shared life with is difficult. Carol and I have been blessed with some very healthy and affirming farewells. When we left China, after nearly seven years at the same university, the other teachers got hundreds of our former students at a gala to celebrate our impact on campus. It was nothing short of precious. We had developed many close friendships on and off campus. You have already heard me reference Yang and Zhou. Leaving them was one of the most difficult good-byes ever for us. Were there tears in all of the good-byes? Of course! But this powerful marking of the end of a season in our lives and ministry helped us to see how God had been at work in and through us. When we left Hong Kong, the church where we served blessed us with a send-off complete with a special rocking chair (one of my happy places). And I have already detailed some of how it went when we left Thailand.

Why is it good to say good-bye? In part, saying good-bye is good because it gives us an opportunity to reflect on what was done before leaving. This, in turn, helps us to look forward to what will be done after we've left. I was the Area Leader for Mainland Southeast Asia for twelve years. In Pioneers, that is a very long time to be in the same leadership position. The time had come for others to bring their leadership skills and impact into the

2. Pink, *Attributes of God*, 60.

area. Rather than feeling like I was abandoning the seventeen teams I looked over, I was entrusting them into God's hands and preparing to watch what new ways God would use them to unfold. When we left, God didn't.

But leaving does take a toll on both sides, on those leaving and those remaining. This period of transition must be proactively addressed. Leaving teammates and national partners and friends exacts a strong emotional toll. Perhaps those who pay the price as much as anyone are our children. It was hard for us to take our daughters away from their friends and familiar places. One of the resources that helped us tremendously was the RAFT metaphor detailed in *Third Culture Kids: Growing Up among Worlds*.[3] In this metaphor, four areas of intentionality are detailed:

R = Reconciliation, making sure that each person leaves with relationships in as good a place as possible

A = Affirmation, being careful to say "Thank you" to those who have impacted you along the way

F = Farewell, saying "Good-bye" to people, pets, possessions, and places

T = Think destination, planning what the exit and re-entry will look like

Building a transitional "raft" helps to minimize the emotional trauma of leaving and reentering. This is true for both temporary departures, such as Home Assignment, or permanent departures. When we leave, we often focus so much on ourselves and our needs that we neglect the impact on those we leave behind, whether they are expats or nationals.

Again, do we trust the Holy Spirit to watch over those we leave behind? If so, we need to communicate that. If God truly is Immanuel (God with us), then we need to live out that reality. When we are tempted to think that those we are leaving behind do not know enough yet, we are actually expressing our fear that God is not near enough to them to guide them. Are we attempting to entrust them into God's hands or into our preparation? In this case, it should be a both/and proposition, not an either/or.

In the end, the issue is one of our faith in God's ability to be good and near to us and to those we leave behind.

How does your faith influence the way you think about having left these people, places, things, and aspects of culture?[4]

---

3. Pollock et al., *Third Culture Kids*, ch. 13.

4. Chaplin, *Returning Well*, 87.

QUESTIONS

1. What fears can you identify as you prepare to leave your ministry? How does God's goodness speak to those fears?

2. This would be a good time to rehearse how some of God's other attributes come to bear on your leaving.

3. Can you remember a time when you had to say a difficult good-bye? What made it difficult? What might you have done differently?

4. How near to God do you feel right now? What could you do to better realize God's nearness?

Chapter 13

Sabbath Lifestyle

God Is Eternal, so Take a Long-term View in How You Rest

"Come to me, all you who are weary and burdened, and I will give you rest." (Matt 11:28)

"Since God is eternal, He can be and continue forever to be the one safe home for His time-driven children."

—A. W. Tozer[1]

WE CALL OUR HOME Gilgal. In 1990, I preached through the book of Joshua at the international church in Shanghai. In that book, Gilgal became a base camp for Israel. They left from there for the southern campaign and came back there before the northern campaign. For Israel, Gilgal became a place to rest and get ready for the next battle. That is why we have called our home Gilgal for the past thirty years. My wife is exceedingly gifted in hospitality, and our whole family has enjoyed having people in our home. It is our desire that those who come into our home will leave better prepared to walk with God on the next steps of their journey for him.

---

1. Tozer, *Knowledge of the Holy*, 40.

What I have often seen is how our visitors, especially those coming from difficult cross-cultural contexts, frequently follow a familiar pattern. The first morning after they arrive, they sleep in a little. The second day, even later. What we observe is their bodies telling them that this is a safe place, a place where they can relax and rest. As mentioned in chapter 5, I sometimes describe it as the feeling one sometimes experiences in the dentist's office. The vest one wears for X-rays becomes comfortable, or at least familiar, until it is taken off. At that moment, a recognition of the weight upon the individual takes place. And when that weight is removed in the areas of emotional and mental stress, relational tension, and spiritual oppression, the physical body wants to shut down for a time of healing and rest.

But here's the problem: cross-cultural workers serving the Lord in difficult places, those who need rest the most, are the ones who often struggle with taking time to rest and rejuvenate. One of the most difficult challenges of my area leader role was getting field workers to take a vacation! I sometimes heard a version of the following: "But the Lord's people are giving the Lord's money for me to do the Lord's work. So I can't take a break." I remember hearing Dr. Howard Hendricks, former professor at Dallas Theological Seminary, share this exhortation at a conference: "One of my students once said to me, 'Well, Dr. Hendricks, you know the devil never takes a vacation.' So I said to him, 'Well, I didn't know he was your role model.'" He went on to share how Jesus modeled rest, both for himself and his disciples.

I also recall how I was guilty of similar thinking. Preparing to go on my first Home Assignment after becoming the Area Leader, I was sitting at a restaurant in Chiang Mai, Thailand, with Bob, a precious brother who was then serving with Barnabas, International. He asked me what my plan for my Area Leader duties was during my Home Assignment. I explained how I delegated a few of my duties. But, I continued, I felt that I could handle a lot of the responsibilities by e-mail from the States. He gently rebuked me for this thinking. In addition to robbing me of the benefits of disengaging, he pointed out that my doing this would model to my team leaders that they too should not plan on disengaging when they would go on their Home Assignments. Ouch! He was right.

Why do we Christians, especially cross-cultural workers, struggle so much with rest? By now, you can easily anticipate my guess with this. It is that we do not have a proper view of God. In this area, I see how an understanding of God's being eternal helps us to trust him enough to stop and rest.

REST IS FOUND IN GOD—"COME UNTO ME"

I do not need to be convinced of my own mortality. My body reminds me of this truth daily. Perhaps it is because of this realization that I push myself to continue to get through my to-do lists and to, less often than I should, stop and smell the roses (or coffee for those of you with that value). Being task-oriented, I find reward in getting things done. It's not that I do not enjoy downtime. But even then, my relaxation often revolves accomplishing Sudoku puzzles, crossword puzzles, and other such activities.

I have allowed myself to believe that, at some level, my worth is determined by how much I get done. When this happens, I am not believing what God says about me—and about him! Now I recognize that some level of stress helps to increase productivity. But there is a time when the increased stress becomes so burdensome that it leads to the mind and body shutting down. I have been at this point a few times, and it is not pretty. I recall one Home Assignment when we came home razor-thin-close to burnout. Thankfully, we were met by an understanding family and church that gave us time to recover and heal, and even encouraged it.

When I work as if I am indispensable, I rob God of his role in my life and ministry. This is not fair to those around me—my family, my team, and those to whom I seek to minister. Those who follow movies that involve armies of any kind, whether *Star Wars*, *Lord of the Rings*, or any military movie, will acknowledge that there are many expendable crewmen or soldiers. These are the ones that may or may not get a credit line at the end. And so it is with us. We are God's expendable crewmen, but we act as though we are generals that cannot take time to rest. (Side note: generals need rest, too.) When we come to realize that we are to give our all for the cause, it does not mean that we do so without giving any consideration to tomorrow's battle. Again referencing Howard Hendricks, he made the distinction when asked about how to live out our lives. When asked if it is better to burn out or to rust out, he replied that it is better to *live* out! His point was that avoiding extremes is preferable to listening to the lie that we must burn ourselves out without a long-term view of service.

Resting in God's Eternality

God is eternal, so I do not have to try to be eternal. I can rest in his eternality. He made it possible for me to enter into an eternal rest as well as temporal rest until I meet him face to face:

> For if Joshua had given them rest, God would not have spoken later about another day. There remains, then, a Sabbath-rest for the people of God; for anyone who enters God's rest also rests from their works, just as God did from his. Let us, therefore, make every effort to enter that rest, so that no one will perish by following their example of disobedience. (Heb 4:8–11)

The operating fear is that we must somehow provide for our own rest from attempting to do works that produce what God has already provided. God promises rest for those who will trust in his provision of Jesus Christ's death and resurrection. Nothing else needs to be added beyond our trust in the sufficiency of the atonement. Clearly, God desires that we rest in him. Rest is important to him. In fact, he modeled it for us when he rested on the seventh day of creation. When he commands us to honor the Sabbath, he is commanding us to live a Sabbath lifestyle. And Jesus himself also modeled this, as he often called his disciples to come apart from ministry to rest.

When we recognize that God is eternal, it helps us to find rest in him. It also helps us to relax and reduce the pressure we sometimes feel to get certain tasks and events accomplished in our time and energy. As Tozer notes,

> The truth is that if the Bible did not teach that God possessed endless being in the ultimate meaning of that term, we would be compelled to infer it from His other attributes, and if the Holy Scriptures had no word for absolute everlastingness, it would be necessary for us to coin one to express the concept, for it is assumed, implied, and generally taken for granted everywhere throughout the inspired Scriptures.[2]

And elsewhere he writes,

> Because God lives in an everlasting now, He has no past and no future. . . . But since God is uncreated, He is not Himself affected by that succession of consecutive changes we call time.[3]

This gives us a sense of stability. God becomes our home.

> Lord, you have been our dwelling place throughout all generations. Before the mountains were born or you brought forth the whole world, from everlasting to everlasting you are God. (Ps 90:1–2)

Scripture exhorts us in this. "Teach us to number our days, that we may gain a heart of wisdom" (Ps 90:12). When we number our days, we gain

2. Tozer, *Knowledge of the Holy*, 38–39.

3. Tozer, *Knowledge of the Holy*, 39.

wisdom from God about how to use the days he gives us. It also helps us to run to him when we are feeling stressed and weary. "Since God is eternal, He can be and continue forever to be the one safe home for His time-driven children."[4]

In order to develop this dependence on our eternal God, we need to humble ourselves:

> For this is what the high and exalted One says—he who lives forever, whose name is holy: "I live in a high and holy place, but also with the one who is contrite and lowly in spirit, to revive the spirit of the lowly and to revive the heart of the contrite." (Isa 57:15)

We humble ourselves when we see God for who he is, high and exalted. He lives forever, so we can trust him to live his eternal purpose through our finite lives. This, in turn, should help us to step back and live in our finiteness. This includes developing a plan for rest.

"OUR HOPE FOR YEARS TO COME"

I am in my early sixties as I type this. And I unapologetically confess that I love the depth of theology and comfort found in many hymns. One of those hymns is the one that Lancaster Bible College plays from the bell tower as a call to chapel. Isaac Watts's "O God, Our Help in Ages Past" is based on Psalm 90. In this hymn, I am reminded of how God's being eternal brings hope in the midst of stormy and stressful episodes of my journey with God:

> O God, our Help in ages past, our Hope for years to come,
> our Shelter from the stormy blast, and our eternal Home.
> Under the shadow of Thy throne Thy saints have dwelt secure;
> sufficient is Thine arm alone, and our defense is sure.
> Before the hills in order stood or earth received its frame,
> from everlasting Thou art God, to endless years the same.
>
> A thousand ages in Thy sight are like an ev'ning gone,
> short as the watch that ends the night before the rising sun.
> Time, like an ever-rolling stream, bears all its sons away;
> they fly forgotten, as a dream dies at the op'ning day.
> O God, our Help in ages past, our Hope for years to come,
> be Thou our Guide while life shall last, and our eternal Home!

4. Tozer, *Knowledge of the Holy*, 40.

Because God is "our eternal Home," we can rest in him at any and all times. But we need to take the time to actually rest in him.

Whether it is heading to your passport country for a Home Assignment or simply a daily or weekly time to disengage, you need to find time to rest. Rest is not simply not doing what you were doing, though that is a good start; true rest will be much more intentional. Just as the desert fathers preached "pray until you pray," so we often need to rest until we truly rest.

Part of developing a Sabbath lifestyle is daily setting aside time to reflect. Typically, we from the West do not do this well. One method is to incorporate the prayer of Examen. This is typically done at the end of the day to prayerfully ask God to shine his light on the day with the intent of becoming aware of how we saw God at work or when we missed seeing him at work. Doing this slows us down and prepares us for a restful sleep before taking on the challenges and opportunities of the next day. In the next chapter, I will discuss the value of debriefing and being honest before God and others as you process longer periods of time on the field.

Rest also involves doing that which restores you—physically, emotionally, and spiritually. The desire to help others find restoration helps drive our hospitality ministry. As mentioned at the beginning of the chapter, this is one of Carol's spiritual gifts. When people come into our home, her gifting is on full display. It may be the way the home is decorated and arranged in such a way as to invite community. Or it may be the smells of her cooking. Or it may be her counseling skills that help those who sit in her presence to feel her genuine care for them. For more than thirty years, Gilgal has been a place for God to use us to care for others.

When God brings opportunities for you to be blessed by those who love God and love you, do not pass them by. Allow yourselves to be cared for by others. You do not always have to be the one seeking to bless others. It is acceptable to be the pampered ones from time to time. And dare I even suggest the following? How about making your needs known so that others can respond? Many cross-cultural workers are so committed to meeting the needs of others that they fail to identify their own needs and to seek God's provision for those needs being met in those around them.

Since God is eternal, his goals/plans/desires never change. The purpose of the church remains to glorify him and to make him known. And just as he calls forth laborers for the fields ripe for harvest, so he calls those same workers to come apart from time to time. May you rest in God's eternality, knowing that he will always be there. He never rests, in part, so that we can.

QUESTIONS

1. What lies do you hear in your mind when you push rest to the side?
2. What does deep rest look like for you?
3. How does God's being eternal impact your ability to rest?
4. How can you provide a place of rest for those around you?

Chapter 14

Debriefing

God Knows Us Intimately, so He Can Be Trusted with Our Deepest Thoughts and Feelings.

"You have searched me, LORD, and You know me." (Ps 139:1)

"Whatever may befall us, God knows and cares as no one else can."

—A. W. TOZER[1]

AT THE END OF *The Return of the King*, the final movie of The *Lord of the Rings* trilogy (based on the books written by J. R. R. Tolkien), is the scene when the Hobbits return to their home, the Shire. Frodo, Samwise, Meriadoc (Merry), and Peregrin (Pippin) peacefully ride into the tranquil Shire with the shared experience of their adventures to save Middle Earth. As they sit in the local pub, they realize that nobody in their hometown has any clue as to what they have gone through. But there, at their table, is a common bond forged from a shared experience. Without words, they recognize how special each one of them will be to each other. And then Samwise begins the process of reengaging with the Shire when he approaches the barmaid whom he intends to marry. Life will never be the same, but it also must move on.

1. Tozer, *Knowledge of the Holy*, 57.

"Nobody understands me." It is not unusual to feel this way when you return from your cross-cultural experience. It is important to find one or more people with whom you can share your thoughts and feelings. This may be to celebrate what God has done, or it may be to begin to find healing and restoration from times of pain and loss.

God has blessed Carol and me with many opportunities to debrief cross-cultural workers returning to their passport countries. Most recently, we met with a couple back from Central America for a two-month Home Assignment. Hearing them talk serves as a reminder of how important it is to provide opportunities to tell the stories of what God is doing in and through them. The joys and struggles are real and need to be shared in a safe place.

When Paul and Barnabas returned to Antioch from the first missionary journey, they experienced some of this:

> From Attalia they sailed back to Antioch, where they had been committed to the grace of God for the work they had now completed. On arriving there, they gathered the church together and reported all that God had done through them and how he had opened a door of faith to the Gentiles. And they stayed there a long time with the disciples. (Acts 14:26–28)

But let us be careful to distinguish between reporting and debriefing. Reporting is typically giving an account of what has happened. It is at the head level. On the other hand, debriefing is a heart-level telling of how you have been impacted by all that has happened. All too often, churches expect to hear about all that the cross-cultural worker has done to further the Great Commission. Sadly, these same committees and elder boards lack the ability or desire to go to the heart level with the cross-cultural worker. This leaves their precious servants of God wondering if anybody cares about them or if anyone is even interested in knowing their struggles. Even worse, sometimes those struggles are left bottled up inside for fear of losing financial support. Where can they turn to for care? The answer, of course, is the Lord. But who else might the Lord use to wrap his loving arms around those who may be feeling broken?

At the end of chapter 4, when discussing the cross-cultural worker's departure, I said that God is both aware and able. He is aware of the challenges we face, and he is able to work through us to make his purposes a reality. In a similar way, he is aware of the struggles we carry, and he is able to walk us through the valley of healing. We can trust him because he knows all things and since he knows us intimately. And he rejoices with us when we praise him publicly for all he has done in and through us.

GOD KNOWS ALL ABOUT ME—"YOU ARE FAMILIAR WITH ALL MY WAYS"

God is omniscient. This means he knows all things, and all things and people are known by him. In times of reflection, it is helpful and comforting to know that we do not inform God of anything. As Tozer writes,

> And to us who have fled for refuge to lay hold upon the hope that is set before us in the gospel, how unutterably sweet is the knowledge that our Heavenly Father knows us completely.[2]

In the previous chapter, I referenced Hebrews 4:9–11 in connection with rest. Just two verses later, we read the following: "Nothing in all creation is hidden from God's sight. Everything is uncovered and laid bare before the eyes of him to whom we must give account." On the one hand, we might be fearful of giving an account to God of all of my thoughts and emotions. On the other hand, it is greatly comforting to know that I can give an account to an all-knowing and loving God (Pss 139:2–4, 23–24).

His ability to lead me in the way everlasting is, in part, based on his knowing all things in general, and all things about me in particular. I find it reassuring to know that I am known deeply by God. And it seems as though being known by others is a high value for us. "Great is our Lord and mighty in power; his understanding has no limit" (Ps 147:5). A great example of this is when Jesus restored Peter (John 21:17). I wonder if Peter took comfort in knowing that Jesus knew his heart, that he truly did love his Lord. Even during this restoration encounter, Peter trusted that Jesus knew his innermost being. God knows and loves us deeply (Matt 10:29–30; Jer 1:5; Rom 11:33–36).

"And now, do not be distressed and do not be angry with yourselves for selling me here, because it was to save lives that God sent me ahead of you" (Gen 45:5). God knew how he would use the events in Joseph's life to impact others. How do you think he will use the events of this cross-cultural experience in your life to impact those you know? And just as God's prophecies indicate his knowing the beginning from the end, so it is with our lives as well. God knows!

Even when those we tell our stories to don't understand, God does. "He knows the way I take" (Job 23:10). But this is why it is so important to enter into times of debriefing, reflecting, and processing with the understanding that God already knows all. It is also why we need to seek out others who love God and love us and are willing to listen without judgment.

---

2. Tozer, *Knowledge of the Holy*, 57.

DEBRIEFING—TRUSTING GOD (AND OTHERS) TO KNOW MY HEART

As mentioned earlier, debriefing at the end of a term, a short-term trip, or even after a traumatic experience should be done with somebody that is not going to offer advice, judgment, or counsel. It is simply a time to tell your story:

> Debriefing is more than giving a report. It is telling our story, complete with experiences and feelings, from our point of view. It is a verbal processing of past events. It differs from a report, which is a factual sharing of details as objectively, accurately and free from emotion as possible. Debriefing, on the other hand, includes both the facts *and* emotional responses, and invites feedback, including appraisal. Some elements necessary for good debriefing include relationship, responsibility, love, respect, concern, trust, and time. It is better if it is not hurried.[3]

When done well, debriefing will have a number of positive outcomes:

> It promotes processing of events plus feelings.
> It informs interested persons.
> It permits evaluation and other feedback.
> It ends isolation.
> It enhances cohesion, connectedness and team spirit.
> It encourages accountability.
> It facilitates change.
> It provides opportunity for growth through reporting and being heard.
> It stimulates renewed commitment.
> It brings rejoicing and glory to God through shared victories.
> It communicates a powerful message of love, respect, and value.
> It is usually a valuable learning experience for the listener(s) also.

Those offering to debrief you do not need to be trained counselors. They need to be good listeners and good questioners. If you do need the benefit of a counselor, that can be done later. Debriefing can be done in one or more sessions, but they should not be rushed. Your goal is to find someone that will help you tell your story. You need to unpack the baggage you brought back with you from your cross-cultural experience.

It is essential to have trust in the person with whom you are sharing your story. This must include a discussion of confidentiality. You need to

3. Gardner, "Debriefing in Missions Settings," 1 (italics original).

have confidence that what you share is going to be kept in that circle of trust. This will help to share openly and honestly.

And do not be afraid of emotions. As you tell your story, it will be important to allow your emotions to be felt and, as much as possible, expressed. If you trust the listener with your emotions, it will be easier to work through any grief you may be experiencing.

Not all debriefing will be to work through sadness or pain. It can also be a way to celebrate the joys and accomplishments you have experienced. We live in a society where telling stories is often met with others trying to tell their "better" story. It becomes a game of one-upmanship. Hopefully, your listener will resist this urge. It is powerful when somebody enters into your joy with you.

Debriefing as a Step Toward the Future

Trusting God and others with your story is an important step toward preparing yourself for the next step of your journey with God. And then comes the reentry. When you come back from your cross-cultural experience, you are met with the challenge of attempting to reengage with a society and social setting that may or may not be as it was when you left. Just as the Hobbits quickly came to realize, you can never go home, because home is not as it once was—and neither are you!

After debriefing those God brings into our lives to help them in their transition, we attempt to gauge their plan for reentry. Just as entry into their host culture included a season of culture shock, the reentry experience can include a similar sense of disorientation. This may result in feelings of isolation, loss of identity, or superiority. It may also include episodes of excessive criticism. And it is not unusual to be overwhelmed with the many choices faced, especially when you have so many emotions that you are trying to process.

I remember early on one of our Home Assignments going to a fast food restaurant. It was a familiar place to us. But when we got there, we felt the pressure of making many decisions in a short period of time. We weren't ready for that. I recall telling Carol to just focus on the first panel of food choices. Likewise, we often counsel those coming back to the USA to go to a Walmart and to walk through the whole store but without buying anything. The second time through, each member of the family was to choose just one item. This is an attempt to help them ease into the many decisions that seemingly jump up at us when we return. Compare having to choose which kind of rice to buy at an open market in Thailand with having to choose a breakfast cereal at a large grocery store. It can, indeed, be overwhelming.

Just as it is helpful to find a cultural interpreter when you arrive on the field, it can be very helpful to have somebody in your passport culture come alongside of you. I remember how Carol's sister helped us to adjust to debit cards when we came back on another Home Assignment. It was comforting to know that she would not laugh at us when we got concerned at the gas station, wondering if we were going to trip off an alarm when we pulled away from the pump after only using this card.

And to those of you who have returned from the field, are there opportunities for you to come alongside others and to help them to share their stories? Can you be that safe cultural interpreter for those experiencing reentry stress?

God knows you and wants you to trust him with your deepest thoughts and emotions. Processing with him and others will help you to celebrate him and all he has done in and through you as you prepare for your next steps with him.

QUESTIONS

1. How does knowing that God knows everything affect you?

2. Can you identify one or more people in your life whom you can trust with your innermost thoughts and feelings? If so, have you taken advantage of this ministry from them? If not, pray that God would help you to find one.

3. Are you willing to be the person needed to help others tell their stories? In what ways can you grow more in this area?

4. How does your prayer life reflect an understanding of God's omniscience?

Chapter 15

Wrap-up

God Is Knowable, and We Must Make Him Known

"Now this is eternal life: that they know you, the only true God, and Jesus Christ, whom you have sent." (John 17:3)

"The heaviest obligation lying upon the Christian Church today is to purify and elevate her concept of God until it is once more worthy of Him—and of her. In all her prayers and labors this should have first place. We do the greatest service to the next generation of Christians by passing on to them undimmed and undiminished that noble concept of God which we received from our Hebrew and Christian fathers of generations past."

—A. W. Tozer[1]

WHY WAS THIS BOOK written? Because God is worthy of our best. When we send cross-cultural workers, they must be prepared well for what they will encounter. They are entrusted with the greatest message: the gospel. It was written because everyone deserves to hear that gospel message. And it was written to empower those who are preparing to go and those who are helping those preparing to go. In short, this book was written for Jesus Christ, for he is worthy.

1. Tozer, *Knowledge of the Holy*, 4.

So how about you? Where are you in your spiritual journey with the Lord? And how has this book helped you? I have attempted to walk through the stages of cross-cultural ministry and to link one of God's attributes to each. Of course, none of God's attributes can be isolated from the others. But focusing on one at a time might help you to lean on God in particular situations. Regarding his omniscience,

> When we talk about God's knowledge of everything, we're talking about a rational approach to God. There are two ways to approach God: theologically and experientially. You can know God experientially and not know much theology, but it's good to know both. The more you know about God theologically the better you can know Him experientially. . . . The purpose of doctrine is to lead you to see and to know God experientially, to know God for Himself, for yourself.[2]

I started out with a plea to prioritize God. How can we do good works for God before becoming conformed to the image of Christ? And how can we attempt to be conformed to the image of Christ unless we know God in all of his glory? I have pulled Tozer along with me on this journey, leaning heavily on his *The Knowledge of the Holy* in order to emphasize God's many attributes. While no single attribute of God stands alone, a study of each has hopefully helped you to better appreciate God and to lean into him in a fuller way than before. Experiencing God to the best of our ability and to the fullest understanding of who he is becomes our goal.

> And without faith it is impossible to please God, because anyone who comes to him must believe that he exists and that he rewards those who earnestly seek him. (Heb 11:6)

Are you seeking God as earnestly as you can? May God increasingly reveal himself to you so that you, in turn, can reveal him to those he brings into your life path.

QUESTIONS

1. Which of God's attributes is most precious to you today? Why?
2. Which of God's attributes do you think he would like you to consider more than you are now?

2. Tozer and Fessenden, *Attributes of God*, 2:107.

3. If you were to go back through this book, which attributes would you add to each chapter's stage of ministry?

4. How would your prayer life benefit from a deeper understanding of His attributes?

Bibliography

Barker, Kenneth L, ed. *The NIV Study Bible, New International Version*. Grand Rapids: Zondervan Bible, 1985.

Bible.org. "14. God is Love." https://bible.org/seriespage/14-god-love.

Chaplin, Melissa. *Returning Well: Your Guide to Thriving Back "Home" after Serving Cross-culturally*. s.l.: Newtown, 2015.

Chapman, Gary. *The 5 Love Languages: The Secret to Love that Lasts*. Chicago: Northfield, 2015.

"Classification of the Attributes of God." http://www.theopedia.com/Classification_of_the_attributes_of_God.

Darabont, Frank, dir. *The Shawshank Redemption*. 1994. Burbank, CA: Warner Bros. Pictures.

de Poissy, Louis. "Chapter II. Attributes of God in General." https://www3.nd.edu/Departments/Maritain/etext/cp37.html.

DeVries, Brian A. "The Contexts of Contextualization: Different Methods for Different Ministry Situations." *Evangelical Missions Quarterly* 55.4 (October 2019) 11–14.

Elmer, Duane. *Cross-cultural Servanthood: Serving in the World in Christlike Humility*. Downers Grove, IL: InterVarsity, 2006.

Feinberg, John S. *No One Like Him: The Doctrine of God*. Wheaton, IL: Crossway, 2001.

"14. God Is Love." https://bible.org/seriespage/14-god-love.

Galli, Mark. *A Great and Terrible Love: A Spiritual Journey into the Attributes of God*. Grand Rapids: Baker, 2009.

Gardner, Laura Mae, et al. "Debriefing in Missions Settings" http://www.relationshipskills.com/resources/Debriefing-in-Missions-Settings.pdf.

Goforth, Rosalind. *Goforth of China*. Grand Rapids: Zondervan, 1937.

González, Justo L. *Knowing Our Faith: A Guide for Believers, Seekers, and Christian Communities*. Grand Rapids: Eerdmans, 2019.

Guinness, Os. *The Call: Finding and Fulfilling the Central Purpose of Your Life*. Nashville: Thomas Nelson, 2003.

Hale, Thomas, Jr., and Gene Daniels. *On Being a Missionary*. Revised edition. Pasadena, CA: William Carey Library, 2012.

Henrichsen, Walter. *Disciples Are Made Not Born: Helping Others Grow to Maturity in Christ*. Colorado Springs: David C. Cook, 2011.

Hesse, Eric. "Every Believer a Missionary." http://sentness.com/2013/05/08/every-believer-a-missionary/.

Hesselgrave, David. *Communicating Christ Cross-culturally*. Second edition. Grand Rapids: Zondervan, 1991.

Kasper, Cindy. *Daily Bread*. Grand Rapids: RBC Ministries, 2014.

Koning, Otto. "The Pineapple Story." http://ministry2kenya.blogspot.com/2017/09/the-pineapple-story-by-otto-koning.html.

MacArthur, John. "God's Absolute Sovereignty." http://www.gty.org/resources/Articles/A167/Gods-Absolute-Sovereignty.

McNicol, Bruce, et al. *The Cure: What if God Isn't Who You Think He Is and Neither Are You?* Phoenix: Trueface, 2016.

Pink, Arthur W. *The Attributes of God*. Blacksburg, VA: Wilder, 2008.

Pollock, David C., et al. *Third Culture Kids: Growing Up among Worlds*. 3rd edition. Boston: Nicholas Brealey, 2017.

Sills, M. David. *The Missionary Call: Find Your Place in God's Plan for the World*. Chicago: Moody, 2008.

Snider, Andy. "Story and System: Why We Should Not Categorize the Attributes of God." https://www.academia.edu/2131858/Story_and_System_Why_We_Should_Not_Categorize_the_Attributes_of_God.

Sproul, R. C. *Essential Truths of the Christian Faith—100 Key Doctrines in Plain Language*. Carol Stream, IL: Tyndale, 1992.

Steffen, Tom A. *Passing the Baton: Church Planting that Empowers*. La Habra, CA: Center for Organizational & Ministry Development, 1997.

Stephens, Elliot D. "Retention and Onboarding: Are We Ready to Ask the Hard Questions?" *Evangelical Missions Quarterly* 55.4 (October 2019) 15–18.

Stetzer, Ed. "Church Planting Series: Creating a Culture of Multiplication." *Christianity Today*, October 2, 2019. https://www.christianitytoday.com/edstetzer/2019/october/church-planting-series-creating-culture-of-multiplication.html

———. "Church Planting Series: How Can Your Church Get Involved in Church Planting?" *Christianity Today*, September 25, 2019. https://www.christianitytoday.com/edstetzer/2019/september/church-planting-series-how-can-your-church-get-involved-in-.html.

———. "Church Planting Series: Should Churches 'Plant Pregnant' Today?" *Christianity Today*, September 24, 2019. https://www.christianitytoday.com/edstetzer/2019/september/church-planting-series-should-churches-plant-pregnant.html.

———. "Church Planting Series: So What Does Church Planting Actually Look Like?" *Christianity Today*, October 3, 2019. https://www.christianitytoday.com/edstetzer/2019/october/church-planting-series-so-what-does-church-planting-actuall.html.

———. "Church Planting Series: Why Don't We Plant?" *Christianity Today*, September 18, 2019. https://www.christianitytoday.com/edstetzer/2019/september/church-planting-series-why-dont-we-plant.html.

Stone, Brian. "Incommunicable Attributes." http://bstoneblog.com/2010/03/22/-incommunicable-attributes/.

Tozer, A. W. *The Knowledge of the Holy: The Attributes of God: Their Meaning in the Christian Life*. New York: HarperCollins, 1961.

Tozer, A. W., and David E. Fessenden. *The Attributes of God*. Vol. 2. 2 vols. Camp Hill, PA: Wing Spread, 2007.

Wellman, Jack. "Quotes about Church." https://www.christianquotes.info/quotes-by-topic/quotes-about-church/#participants-list-1.

"Westminster Shorter Catechism." https://www.apuritansmind.com/westminster-standards/shorter-catechism/.

www.ingramcontent.com/pod-product-compliance
Lightning Source LLC
Chambersburg PA
CBHW060345100426
42812CB00003B/1130